BLISTERING BARBECUES

641.76

OVER 150 RECI HEROES

BLISTERING
BARBECUES

OVER 150 RECIPES FROM THE AL FRESCO HEROES

KATE TUNNICLIFF
NIGEL TUNNICLIFF
TIM REEVES

Absolute

First published in Great Britain in 2004 by
Absolute Press
Scarborough House
29 James Street West
Bath BA1 2BT
Phone 44 (0) 1225 316013
Fax 44 (0) 1225 445836
E-mail info@absolutepress.co.uk
Website www.absolutepress.co.uk

Reprinted June 2004

**Photography: David Betteridge
(except cover photo and page 119,
by Simon Smith)**

A catalogue record of this book is available
from the British Library

ISBN 1 904573 13 4

Printed and bound by Butler and Tanner,
Frome, Somerset

www.blistering.co.uk

CONTENTS

Introduction

Blistering Barbecues was set up by Nigel Tunnicliff, a chef of some 25 years' worldwide experience, and party-throwing impresario-chef Tim Reeves. Nigel and Tim met over falafels and veggie curries on Nigel's award-winning Red Leb stall at the Glastonbury Rock Festival in the mid-nineties. They hatched the Blistering plan to the marquee-shaking thud of the Pyramid Stage. They had found a hole in the outside catering market and they were going to fill it.

Blistering kicked off in 1998 with four barbecues and a third-hand transit van. Now in our eighth year of trading, with a battery of 26 six-foot barbecues and 6 half-ton wood-fired ovens, Blistering Barbecues travel all over the country and have now enjoyed some successful forays overseas, as far as Sri Lanka. We have learnt a thing or two about how to create delicious food *al fresco*. Our recipes really do work – they have to when you are conjuring food for up to 5,000 guests ready for a party. And we're not talking just barbecued bangers and burgers. From king prawns to tuna; from sirloin steaks to ostrich; from chicken thighs to geese roasted in the wood-fired oven; we've done it all – over and over again. As outside caterers, we take the party to wherever the client wants it; be that on the balcony of a 29th floor City penthouse, or down the muddy track, across the stream and up the hill to some ruined Scottish castle.

We didn't get to where we are today without the occasional behind-the-scenes drama. It always works out beautifully in the end, but when you're in a business that depends on staff, hire equipment and ingredients turning up on time, vehicles never breaking down and the British sun always shining, a calm, adaptable and understanding temperament is a prerequisite.

It's through seasons of resounding successes as well as through the occasional drama, that we have evolved the most reliable, foolproof recipes and infallible wood-roasting and grilling techniques. We have piled all of this experience, not only into this book, but into developing and honing the slickest most versatile barbecue around; the 'Blistering Barbecue'. In our travels, we have also tracked down a sensational piece of kit, the Portuguese 'Blistering Beehive Wood-fired Oven'.

And we've found the best charcoal. At Blistering, we are charcoal purists. The succulence and flavour of beautiful ingredients charcoal-grilled or wood-roasted is unsurpassable. You don't have to road test any of the charcoal; we've done it for you. Go straight for British handmade charcoal. It generates great heat, lights easily, is virtually smoke-free and lasts well (*see* page 12).

We love *al fresco* food: that's why we're in the business. The combination of hot grills and wood-roasts with cool crunchy salads and mellow roast vegetables served with a choice of sauces is heaven on a plate for us. At Blistering, it's all about flavour. You can forget the common story of the average supermarket chicken thigh destined for half-cremation on the British back garden

barbecue; chucked into a trolley on a Friday evening and shoved into a fridge without a further thought, beyond 'job done', the thigh sits there, unmarinated, to be wrenched beerily from its wrappings the following day and plonked onto a smoking barbecue, ice cold and unseasoned. Ignored by everyone, it emerges black on one side, beige on the other and pink in the middle. You may not recognise all of this, but some of it rings true doesn't it? Well those days are over.

Every recipe in this book has evolved in the field. Thanks to the inspired international brigade of chefs we attract to our payroll, experimentation and authentic twists to ingredients lists here and there over the years have produced memorable flavours and true reliability. As well as covering meats, birds, fish, vegetables and salads, we have included a sizeable chapter of over 40 sauces, salsas and relishes. Any Blistering buffet is held together by an appropriate selection of these delicious lubricants. Once you have tried some of the recipes, it's over to you to carry on experimenting. This is how the greatest recipes are discovered.

But we don't only give you our recipes, we advise you on the practical essentials of *al fresco* cooking. We take you through the *Blistering Kit* (*see* pages 10-15) from British Handmade Charcoal to top tongs. In *Blistering Know-How* (*see* pages 18-28), we steer you expertly through the simple-when-you-know-how processes of charcoal barbecuing; from marinating to lighting your coals or wood and from finding your ingredients, to presenting the finished product. We introduce the concept of 'Top Shelf' ingredients. We also give you the beginners' guide to roasting in the wood-fired oven.

So, if you happen to be one of those guests who have hung out by our barbecues checking out techniques, equipment and asking for recipes, here is the book with all the answers.

BLISTERING KIT

BLISTERING
KNOW-HOW

Slaving over a hot stove is quite literally what we have been doing for years. Here's the lowdown on the essential kit we recommend you have to hand before you light up.

Barbecues

The Blistering Barbecue

Barbecue designs come in all shapes, sizes and prices. Some years back at Blistering, we were asked to test a selection of barbecues for a magazine. We found that although some of them were fine, and certainly looked great, none of them grilled with the flexibility of our own Blistering design. The Blistering secret is in the ease with which you can control the height of the food above the coals. With this system, it is simple to avoid that old barbecue cliché of the outside of your food being burnt before the inside is cooked. Not wanting to miss a trick, we set about the process of designing a modern back-garden-friendly version of our own trade barbecue.

Four years on, the result is 'The Blistering Barbecue'. We make no apology for shameless plugging. With our years of grilling experience, we have not only produced a great looking barbecue, but one that is very user-friendly and will produce perfectly cooked food every time.

The Blistering Beehive Wood-fired Oven

Wood-fired ovens have now become commonplace in pizza restaurants round the country. We discovered this little beauty in Portugal in our second year at Blistering. Before we knew it, we had purchased six of the larger half tonne ovens and were carting them around the country. The ovens have become as indispensable as the barbecues at Blistering with the amazing flavour they add to almost any type of food. As well as producing crisp succulent whole fish, tender and juicy sirloins and the best ever roast potatoes, the ovens have been rolled out for umpteen memorable summer pizza parties both at work and at home with our families and friends. Nigel even cooked his Christmas Goose and all the trimmings in his oven last year. Now that's dedication!

Gas Barbecues

We appreciate why gas barbecues have become so popular over the years. It's like having a gas oven in your back garden. They are seen as being quick to light, controllable and hassle free. Although all the cooking methods in this book are geared up for the charcoal barbecue, any of the recipes featured can be cooked on gas.

If we don't sound very excited about gas, it's because we aren't. You simply don't get the same depth of flavour as with wood and charcoal. And there's no fire – where's the fun in that? We aren't trying to be cooking snobs here, it's just the way we feel.

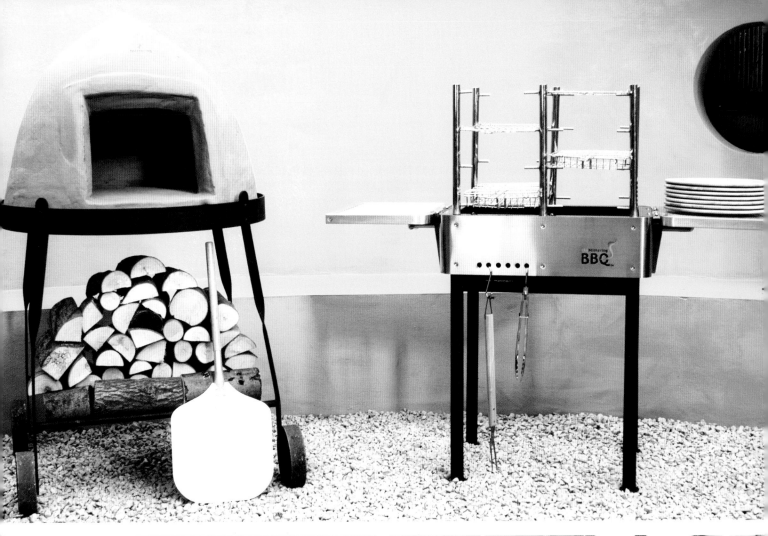

Charcoal

Fire-lighting is a passion for us and we have it down to an art. Man has been lighting fires for millennia, so why go out and buy a gas barbecue now, when charcoal barbecuing is so easy, so dramatic and provides you with hugely superior *al fresco* dishes?

Charcoal – why we buy British!

Getting in the right type of charcoal really does make a difference to successful cooking.

When buying your charcoal watch out for the quality – it varies immensely. Much of the cheaper charcoal available at supermarkets and petrol stations is not great. It can be hard to light and when lit, smokes for a long time. It may burn with great heat, but can also die a very sudden death.

From the early days at Blistering, we started using British charcoal, not because we were really aware of the eco-issues concerned, but because of its quality. British charcoal is almost smoke-free, white hot and ready for grilling in 20 minutes and burns at a high temperature for a good hour. For years, our friend Donald Macleod from Henley (*see* Suppliers' appendix, p215) has been making his fortnightly night-time deliveries to our Battersea headquarters with tonnes of his top grade British charcoal. We love the stuff!

Over the years, we have got to know a lot more about the people involved in making and promoting British charcoal. Jenny Martin, a consultant specializing in the marketing of sustainably produced local timber, told us why British charcoal is best:

'Local charcoal is mostly produced using traditional techniques that work in harmony with woodland ecosystems – a sustainable fuel from a renewable source – coppiced woodlands. When you buy charcoal from a local producer using sustainable methods, you are investing in the rural community in Britain, providing financial incentive for well managed woodlands, and minimizing the quantity of fuel used to

The use of charcoal in Europe can be traced back at least 5,500 years. It was the smelting fuel of the bronze and iron ages.

The wood we use to make this charcoal comes from sustainably managed broadleaf woodlands. These woods are either being thinned or coppiced. This method of woodland management has been practised in Britain for centuries. All our broadleaf trees will regenerate or will be replanted, enabling us to look after the environment and wildlife, and help us to stop imported charcoal that may have come from Rainforests or unsustainable wood!

In buying this pro...
and...

transport that charcoal to your barbecue. The transport of local charcoal uses only 15% of the energy required for charcoal imports from tropical sources. Furthermore, it is often impossible to tell if imported charcoal has been produced using socially and environmentally acceptable methods that do not cause damage to people, communities and eco systems'.

For more information on UK suppliers, log onto the Blistering website at www.blistering.co.uk.

Eco-Friendly Charcoal

If you want to go completely eco-friendly you can do it with Greenheat briquettes. They are made from olive stone and burn hot and slow. Most supermarkets stock Greenheat over the summer months now. They also produce a good fire starter gel made from sugar cane. *See* www.greenheat.com for more information.

Wood

Hard woods, such as oak or fruit tree cuttings (apple, pear, plum) are best for both the barbecue and the wood-fired oven. Avoid pine and other evergreen logs; they are too resinous. For extra flavour, soak and add hickory wood chips, woody herbs such as rosemary and thyme or spices such as coriander seeds, star anise or cinnamon sticks to the glowing embers towards the end of any grill time.

Lighting Aids

We understand the convenience of firelighters and liquid lighting aids, but we never use them ourselves. There is no point in buying top quality charcoal only to use a cocktail of chemicals to light it. The only lighting method we use is good old fashion newspaper, kindling and a few small chunks of charcoal. We would also recommend 'chimney' starters for efficient fire lighting. These are metal cylinders, which channel the air directly into the starting fire.

N.B. The lighting stage of the barbecuing process is potentially very dangerous and we urge you to use your common sense. Keep children well away, never use petrol and never pour extra lighter fluid onto the coals once they are lit.

The Tools

At Blistering, we have a comprehensive checklist, which we consult before leaving the unit for every job we do. It comprises anything and everything needed for a successful barbecue party. Maybe you will think that some of the items are unnecessary, but trust us. In their own way, every item listed will make your life easier either in your own kitchen or behind the grills.

In the Kitchen

Spice grinder
Our kitchen is constantly buzzing with the sound of spices being blitzed in one of our spice grinders. A coffee grinder costs little more than a tenner. Buy one to dedicate to spice grinding, as once you've ground up Indian spices in a coffee grinder, that's the end of it for coffee beans.

Pestle and mortar
Ideal for pestos, garlic and fresh herbs. You can often buy terrific stone and terracotta pestle and mortars in oriental stores.

Mandolin or Japanese Mandolin
A number of our salad recipes recommend the use of a mandolin; the piece of kit that allows you to finely slice or matchstick vegetables precisely and quickly. Just watch your fingertips though.

Salad spinner
No one likes wet lettuce.
Also good for drying fresh herbs.

Metal skewers
As used in every kebab shop around the world. Long lasting and brilliant for small pieces of meat, prawns and vegetables, as the metal acts as a heat conductor.

Bamboo skewers
Easy to get hold of in a variety of lengths in oriental stores. Always soak in water for at least 30 minutes before using over the coals. Skewers are always great for Bites, kebab starters and tapas.

Good quality knives, carving knife and fork and sharpening steel
We know from visiting any number of domestic kitchens in the course of our work about the woeful state of most kitchen knives. Just buy a couple of good knives and sharpen them regularly. It's simple really, and makes your life so much easier.

Steak knives
Always use them in restaurants but never quite get round to buying them for the home.

Disposable gloves
We get through thousands of these at Blistering every year. Easily available at supermarkets these days and great to have on hand for messy marinades, raw meat and fish. Not forgetting protection when chilli chopping.

Clingfilm, strong plastic bags and foil
We should take out shares in these items; we go through so much over our busy summer season. Strong plastic bags are great for marinating food in.

And, in no particular order:

Chopping boards Separate ones for raw and cooked meats. A third for chopping vegetables and fruit.
Cocktail sticks
Pizza cutting wheel
Pizza shovel
Poultry shears or good kitchen scissors
Spider A circular mesh scoop
Fish slice
Meat mallet
Rolling pin
Oil brushes
Pans Skillet or frying pan with lid for dry frying spices
Sea salt and pepper grinder
Terracotta or other ovenproof dishes
Whisk

Behind the Barbecue

Fuel
Logs, charcoal, hickory chips, kindling, newspapers, matches and tapers.

Hinged Sandwich Racks
There are endless reasons to invest in some long-handled hinged sandwich racks – *see* page 20.

A couple of good basting brushes
You buy cheap, you buy twice! Watch the brush hair disappear in front of your eyes over the heat unless you invest in a natural hair one.

Wire brush
Essential for cleaning the grill racks. Best results obtained when the racks are hot and smoking just before you start the cooking.

Sacrificial tea towel for oiling hot racks
This will sit next to the barbecue with a small bowl or plastic container of vegetable oil. Before anything is cooked on the barbecue, to prevent food from sticking to the grill bars or hinged sandwich racks, the racks are knocked against the side of the barbecue, brushed with a wire brush and then rubbed down with the lightly oiled rag.

A good work surface next to the barbecue
You can never have enough space so any surface or solid table is recommended. Make sure that it is clean before use. Keep raw ingredients away from finished dishes.

A good pair of tongs
If you can get your hands on a pair, the best tongs on the market are the stainless steel catering tongs with the scalloped edges and the locking device at the hinged end.

Oven mits or plenty of oven cloths
Protect yourself. Essential for hot cooking racks and oven trays.

'Insertion' meat thermometer or digital temperature probe
A thermometer rigged up with a skewer to insert into the meat. We find this an essential bit of kit for ensuring perfectly pink red meat or for checking 'doneness' of chicken and whole fish.

A battered old oven tray
Have one of these on hand warmed for resting small cuts of meat and fish at the side of the barbecue.

Small fire extinguisher and fire blanket
Better looking at them than for them. Occasionally, accidents will happen – believe us!

First aid and burn bandages
Fire and sharp knives = accidents. Invest in plasters and burn bandages.

Small hoe and fire poker
Or something similar for working the hot coals.

Horse hair or natural fibre brush
To brush back the embers from the floor of the wood-fired oven.

Water spray
Will keep food moist while cooking, and will slow down flair ups on fatty meats. If you don't have a Blistering Barbecue, these may be essential.

Lighting
There is nothing worse than not being able to see what you are cooking, or even worse, eating uncooked food because the chef or cook can't see what they are doing. There is so much good portable lighting around these days, just be careful to keep electric leads etc away from the barbecue! Failing that, plenty of candles should do the trick.

For serving
Paper napkins
Disposable plates
Knives and forks

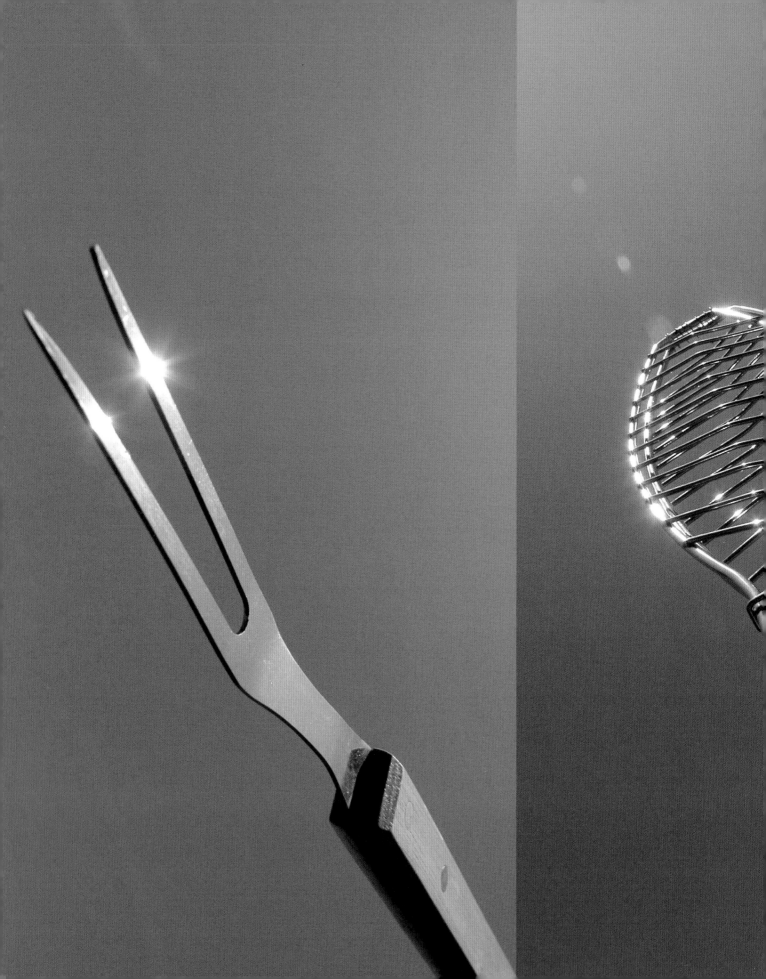

Cooking with fire is dramatic, but it doesn't have to be intimidating. With our years of experience, offering thousands of guests a huge range of grilled foods directly from the barbecue, we feel that you should be confident in picking up some tips from us.

Consign uninspiring chaotic back garden barbecues to history. Think marinade, think embers, think serving and presentation, think theatre.

Now you have the basic equipment, we get the embers up and running and demonstrate the versatility of cooking with charcoal. This is a very simple and natural way to cook once you are organised. Here we tell you how.

A Blistering Party – the rules

Blistering parties fall into a number of formats. We have Blistering Buffets, Blistering Bites Parties, Blistering Tapas Parties, Blistering Pizza Parties, Blistering Grazing Parties and Blistering Sit-down Dinners. All different, all speak for themselves, but we always follow the same rules.

Light the barbecue before the guests arrive

Even have some grilling underway – maybe just a few Bites. At the very least, your guests will arrive to the tantalising smell of the debris burning off the barbecue grills. So often at Blistering parties, even this basic aroma will provoke compliments from the guests.

Be *en place*

The chef's term for having everything in place ready to go. Put aside some time the day before, for marinating and preparing everything to as advanced a state as you can. This will leave you with less washing up and more time to set up drinks and create the party atmosphere on the day. Take all your barbecue ingredients out of the fridge and leave covered to lose the fridge chill before grilling.

Be organised around your barbecue

Have enough work surface. Work out how many grill loads of food you have to cook. What other equipment will you need? Work through the list on page 15. How will you keep raw meat separate from cooked?

Stay with your barbecue

Stay for as long as you are grilling, for the best results and for safety's sake. You won't get lonely. Blistering chefs never do. There are always a handful of – invariably male – guests who huddle around giving our chef's advice. Barbecuing is theatre. Get to know and love your barbecue's idiosyncrasies. Baste lovingly. Watch your dishes grilling, being ready to turn them if oil drips and sets off some flaring and smoking. The grill times quoted within each of our recipes cannot be guaranteed owing to the animal nature of cooking with fire, so watch with care.

Barbecue techniques

How to light your barbecue and sustain it

At Blistering, we do not use firelighters, preferring to stick to newspaper, kindling and matches or tapers. We use British traditionally made charcoal from coppiced woods, or sustainable forests (*see* page 12). Scrunch up 3 or 4 double pages of broadsheet-sized newspaper and place in the barbecue trough under a good handful of kindling. Place a few chunks of charcoal on top and light the paper. When you have a flame from the wood, sprinkle charcoal on the top in a pile like a bonfire. Let this burn for 15-20 minutes with your barbecue rack above it. You are ready to grill when smoking has abated and the embers are glowing. Good quality charcoal will last for up to an hour. If you need to top up with more charcoal, allow the smoke produced by the new charcoal to burn itself out before cooking food above it.

Barbecue temperatures

As barbecuing is not a precise science, the temperature and grill times stipulated within each recipe can only act as guidelines. Grill times are dependent on many factors including weather conditions (wind, damp and air temperature, the age, type and dampness of charcoal and the core temperature of the food). We make an attempt here to calibrate the temperatures for you, but there is no substitute for experience with your own barbecue. Once the charcoal has been burning for 20 minutes or so and is smoke-free and glowing, hold your hand directly over the grill bars and consult the following table. If the temperature does not fall exactly into one of these categories, but is good and hot nevertheless, rake the coals around a little, but don't waste too much time trying to adjust it; just alter the grill time accordingly and use one of the methods for testing for 'doneness' described on pages 22-23. We'll say it again; you need to get to know your own barbecue.

Temperature terminology	How long can you bear to hold your hand directly over the grill?
Slow or 'holding'	Indefinitely, but warm
Medium or 'cook'	6-7 seconds
Medium-high or 'sizzle'	3-4 seconds
High or 'searing'	1 second

Slow or 'holding' temperature
Ideal for keeping food warm, or resting meat (*see* page 23).

Medium or 'cook' temperature
Larger pieces of meat are started off at 'sizzle' temperature and then transferred to medium heat, or 'cook' temperature.

Medium-high or 'sizzle' temperature
Most of the recipes in this book are grilled at medium-high, or 'sizzle' temperature. At this temperature, food will brown; so will need to be turned regularly.

High or 'searing' temperature
Fish, such as tuna, which is best seared on the outside and left pink in the centre should be cooked on high, or at 'searing' temperature. Squid also benefits from extra-quick cooking. If you like your steak 'blue', you should use 'searing' temperature so that the outside chars before the flesh begins to cook through.

Preventing food from sticking to the racks and grill

Clean and lightly oil the grill or racks
Any food will stick on a barbecue if the grill bars or racks are not brushed, cleaned and lightly oiled before use. At Blistering, we lay the grill racks across the barbecue trough as soon as we light the charcoal. When the coals get up to heat, the racks are good and hot, so we pick them up by the handles and knock them against the side of the barbecue to remove any rough debris. We then give them a good going over with a wire brush and, taking great care to keep fingers clear of the hot bars, rub them down with a lightly oiled sacrificial tea towel. You are now ready to grill.

Make sure your grill is up to heat
If it's not your food is sure to stick.

Light oiling of meat, fish or vegetables
If your dish has been subjected to an oil-free marinade, it is important to lightly brush the surfaces of your meat, fish or vegetables with oil before grilling. But take care, as too much oil will lead to flaring, smoking and bitterness.

Turning food on a barbecue
Don't turn your food before it is well grilled or marked on the underside. The charring process essentially burns the meat, fish or vegetable off the grill bars, making it very easy to turn.

Hinged Sandwich Racks
At Blistering, the hinged racks are in constant use. They put us in control of the grilling process in many ways. Heat the rack over the coals. Take away from the heat. Clean as instructed above, load up the rack, close it and place it back on the barbecue.

- They allow you to grill and turn smaller items, such as prawns or sweet potato chips with ease. Instead of fiddling around with tongs, everything will be turned simultaneously.
- They allow you to quickly move your food away from the coals if the barbecue is too hot.
- By placing skewers loaded with meat in hinged sandwich racks, you will prevent individual pieces of meat from swinging round the skewer.
- Your food will be held in shape. Great for stuffed chicken breasts or boned whole chickens.
- No problems turning larger pieces of food, which can difficult to move, such as whole fish.

The 8 Stages to Beautifully Barbecued Food

1 Basic Ingredients

The summer months, when most barbecue bones are tickled, coincide perfectly with the season of fruit and vegetable gluts, leaving you spoilt for great ingredients both to barbecue (sweet corn, courgettes, plums, apples, etc.) and to throw together into great salads to accompany your grilled meats, birds and fish. You should always wash vegetables before use, particularly if you aren't peeling them.

This book features over 50 different marinades. All the ingredients are available in the right shops on the high street. If you're stuck, check out our Suppliers' appendix on p215.

2 Marinating

If you have a fantastic piece of well-hung organic beef from a farm down the road, then yes, maybe just brush it lightly with a little oil, season it with some sea salt and freshly ground black pepper and barbecue it over the coals as is, serving it with any of our sauces (*see* pages 175-196). Otherwise, if like most of us you have just bought a piece of meat, some chicken, fish or vegetables from the shop down the road, then it would be a crime not to steep it in the right marinade.

Marinades don't only flavour meat, but they also tenderise. At Blistering, we are great fans of the overnight marinade. It is a happy coincidence that overnight marinating gives the best flavour and is also convenient for our *mise en place*. It means that we can get everything 'boxed off' and packed up and labelled in the fridge the night before a job. Some more delicate fish and shellfish will not benefit from overnight marinating and never use salt, or lemon and lime juices in a marinade for longer than two hours. Avoid pineapple juice, as it is very destructive, breaking down meat and fish fibres totally.

We arrived at our final marinade recipes through years of experimentation in the field and in our back gardens. Do follow the recipes, but don't hesitate to bring out any flavour more strongly by adding an extra teaspoon or so of this or that here or there. If you don't have some of the ingredients, have a hunt through your shelves and fridge to see what you might use as a substitute. This is how great recipes are created.

Five top tips for marinating

• Marinate overnight whenever possible for maximum flavour (unless stated otherwise in the recipe).

• We love extra virgin olive oil, but never use it in marinades. It burns and smokes on contact with the barbecue. Use light olive oil, or vegetable oil instead and save the good stuff for your salads and sauces.

• Marinate in strong plastic bags, tied securely to prevent leakage when you turn them. Otherwise, always cover food tightly with clingfilm and use non-reactive containers such as glass, or stainless steel.

• Before placing on the barbecue grill, rub or shake off any excess marinade, particularly if there is any oil in it, to prevent burning or flaring and the consequent smoky bitter flavour.

• Never put cooked meat back onto the same dish you used for marinating. Always use a clean serving dish or plate.

3 Seasoning

This is where so many home barbecuers mess up. You'd think it was blindingly obvious, but in fact seasoning is so often neglected. This is one of the first lessons any chef learns. Never add salt to a marinade, unless you are marinating for no more than 2 hours. Pepper is fine overnight, but salt never. Always season with salt just before barbecuing and don't be afraid to season well. Although we are great fans of flaked sea salt, such as Maldon, it will just fall off through the barbecue grill. Either blitz Maldon in your spice grinder, or use fine sea salt.

4 Losing fridge temperature

Always give enough time out of the fridge for raw barbecue dishes to lose their chill and to be approaching room temperature. If the meat, chicken, fish or vegetable is too cold in the centre, the outside may well burn before the inside is cooked through. The following recipe grill times are based on raw dishes being taken out of the fridge at least 20 minutes before barbecuing. To make this easy to remember, unless it is a very hot day, you should think about taking marinating dishes out of the fridge around the time that you are lighting the barbecue.

5 Temperature control during grilling

The key to perfectly barbecued dishes is in temperature control. Temperature control can be achieved in different ways, depending on the barbecue design. The Blistering Barbecue is based around the need to control the proximity of the food to the coals and employs a rack system with three different heights and moveable grills and hinged sandwich racks. Other barbecues may have some degree of height control, or may employ lids to slow things down. Other systems leave you with no option but to shuffle your grilling food around from hot patches to cooler parts of the rack, or to place the food on foil to slow things down.

6 Testing for 'doneness'

A practised hand can feel the 'doneness' or raw fleshiness of meat with a pinch or a poke. However, this method takes years of experience, and though with steak, tuna and lamb, it is not so important, it is essential that pork, chicken, sausages and some fish dishes should be cooked all the way through before serving. The problem is double-edged though. Yes, it's important to cook some dishes all the

way through, but overcooking can leave food dry and unappealing.

We have given grill times in all the recipes to act as a guide, but barbecuing is not an exact science. Your grill time will vary depending on a number of factors including charcoal quality, weather and the core temperature of your raw ingredients. So how do you know when your food is cooked? There are a number of solutions. At Blistering, we standardise cooking of larger joints using temperature probes. Alternatively, using a small sharp knife, cut into the centre of the meat, (down to the bone if there is one) to check that the flesh is cooked and juices are running clear. For flaky fish, such as salmon, press the flesh with your finger or a fork to check that the flakes come apart.

7 Resting the meat

Resting meats after barbecuing is as essential a part of the barbecuing process as any other. If you were to eat a steak directly off the barbecue, it would be tough and juices would flow out the moment you prodded it with your steak knife. Leaving it to rest for a few minutes allows the meat sinews to relax and reabsorb the juices. At Blistering, we rest the meat on a warmed tray on the top rack or away from the direct heat of the Blistering Barbecue, covered with perforated foil. Why perforated? While you want to keep the meat warm, you don't want it to steam and overcook in its own juices. We often squeeze lime or lemon juice over meat while it is resting to improve flavour and to further tenderise.

8 Presentation

Although the food is the real star of any Blistering party, we didn't get where we are today without making an effort with the presentation. Half of our Battersea unit is taken up with shelves of original funky plates, trays and props. We are constantly involved with themed parties from Cuban to Malaysian, from underwater to ultraviolet and from Bollywood to Harry Potter. You'll probably find that more often than not, a pile of plates, forks and paper napkins will suffice, but if you're looking for that extra 'wow' factor, look out for special platters and decorate your table to set the scene. Use fabrics, branches, flowers, candles, flashing lights – anything. Use your imagination and scour the house, garden and high street. Just make sure that all your decoration is done before the grilling begins.

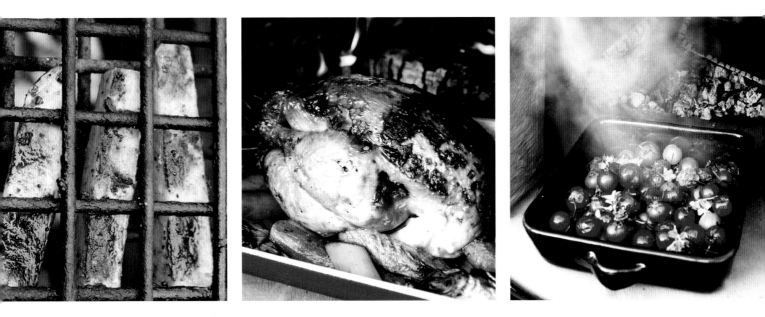

A Beginner's Guide to Using the Blistering Beehive Wood-fired Oven

We use our wood-fired ovens as much at home as at work. Once you've tried meats, fish, vegetables and pizzas cooked this way, we hope that you'll be hooked too. As with barbecuing, you need to get to know your own oven and develop your own techniques. Put in the mileage and you will be rewarded with delicious food time and time again.

The fire burns towards the back of the oven. With the pointed beehive shape, the flame licks up the back of the oven and then down into the centre, generating enormous heat at the heart of the oven. Once the fire is up and going, you can either roast food very quickly in the hotter central area on the raised metal stand or 'trivet', or you can slow things down on the floor at the front of the oven where it is a little cooler. Often, you will start the cooking and browning process on the trivet, moving your dish to the cooler floor of the oven to cook it through.

Your logs must be hard wood and definitely not the more resinous evergreen. They must be dry, and well seasoned. Log size will vary, but should measure in the region of 25 x 8 x 8cm.

How to light and maintain the fire

Never use firelighters in a wood-fired oven. The chemicals will seep into the terracotta.

Tightly scrunch up four or five pieces of broadsheet-sized newspaper and place them in the middle of your oven. Top with six or seven sticks of kindling. We like to scatter on a few chunks of charcoal as well, as once lit, they help the larger logs to catch. Light the newspaper in four places; first at the back, then on each side and finally at the front. Let the fire take a hold of the kindling and the charcoal (if using) and place a few small logs on the top. Allow the fire to establish itself well before pushing it gently to the back of the oven, using a rake or a poker. You need to maintain a small flame, so as the fire dies down, you add another log. How often you need to stoke up your fire depends on a whole number of factors, but you'll probably find yourself throwing another small log on every 20-30 minutes or so.

How to control the temperature

As we have said, you need to maintain a small flame that licks up the back of the oven and down towards the trivet. If the fire rages too strongly, the flame with curl across the roof of the oven and lick out of the door, maybe even claiming your eyebrows in the process. If the fire is too lively, using a poker, spread out and knock the logs around to calm the flames. Alternatively, add another log or a sprinkling of charcoal.

Stay with your oven

Your oven can build up a very intense heat and so cook very quickly. We urge you to stay with your oven. You may need to turn your food regularly, or cover it with foil to slow things down. Always have an oven-proof cloth to hand.

The Blistering Top Shelf

The term 'Top Shelf' came about in our kitchens as the chefs raided the shelves of the Blistering dry stores for various ingredients to make up marinades and sauces. From tomato ketchup to horseradish sauce, from Cola to sloe gin, from cumin to saffron; they all have a place in Blistering marinades. What have you got in your kitchen cupboard? We bet that it's stacked with tasty stuff you've forgotten about. Here's a pretty exhaustive list of the Blistering basic Top Shelf.

Asian/Indian

- **Dried spices and herbs**
  Cumin, coriander, fennel and fenugreek seeds, cinnamon sticks, whole nutmeg, cloves, chilli flakes, cayenne pepper, mustard seeds (black and white), cracked black pepper, whole peppercorns (black, white and green), cardamom pods, curry leaves, ground ginger, turmeric, garam masala
- Mild curry powder
- Mango powder
- Onion powder
- Garlic powder
- Mango chutney
- Tamarind paste

Oriental

- Banana leaves
- Coconut milk, cream and powder
- Chinese five spice
- Star anise
- Mirin
- Fish sauce (nam pla)
- Oyster sauce
- Palm sugar
- Rice vinegar
- Shrimp – dried
- Soy sauce
- Sweet soy sauce (Indonesian ketjap manis)
- Szechwan peppercorns
- Thai curry pastes
- Wasabi
- Sesame oil
- Sesame seeds
- Hoi sin sauce
- Plum sauce
- Pickled ginger – pink
- Teriyaki sauce
- Sesame seeds

Middle Eastern

- Caraway seeds
- Saffron
- Paprika
- Pinenuts
- Pomegrate powder
- Pomegranate molasses
- Pomegranate juice
- Pickled green chillies
- Ground sumac
- Tahini

Mediterranean

- Capers
- Olive oil
- Extra virgin olive oil
- **Flavoured olive oils**
  garlic, rosemary, etc.
- Anchovies
- Green peppercorns in brine

Off License

- Beer
- Brandy
- Cider
- Red and white wine
- Madeira or sherry
- Pernod
- Stout
- Port
- Sloe gin
- Vodka
- Kirsch
- Amaretto

Deli or Supermarket

- Australian lemon myrtle
- Coca-Cola
- Chipotle chillies (tinned)
- **Dried Herbs**
  Thyme, sage, oregano
- **Dried spices and salts**
  Allspice, celery salt, fine and flaked sea salt
- **Freshly Ground Pepper**
  black and white
- Honey – runny
- Horseradish sauce
- Maple syrup
- Marmalade – Seville orange
- Mint Jelly
- **Mustards**
  dried, Dijon, English, American Hot Dog
- Seeds
- Sea salt

- **Seeds**
  Poppy, pumpkin and sunflower
- **Sugar**
  white, soft brown, muscavado
- Tabasco
- Tinned plum tomatoes
- Tomato ketchup
- Tomato purée
- Vegetable oil
- **Vinegars**
  White wine, balsamic
- Worcestershire Sauce

And these always to hand...

- Cajun Seasoning (*see* page 64)
- Jerk Seasoning (*see* page 33)
- Red Leb Paste (*see* page 48)
- Blistering Sweet Chilli Sauce (*see* page 187)
- Blistering Edible Glitter (via mail order from the Blistering website, www.blistering.co.uk)

BITES

Orange Sweet Potato Chips with Cajun Seasoning served with Sour Cream & Chives

MAKES 50-60 BITES

- Instant marinade or overnight

- A hinged sandwich rack is pretty much essential here.

1kg orange sweet potatoes
2 tbsp olive oil
1 heaped tbsp Cajun seasoning
   (*see* recipe in Cajun Chicken Sandwich, page 64)
fine sea salt
Sour Cream & Chives (*see* page 190)
fresh coriander, chopped, or to taste

Scrub the sweet potatoes, leaving the skin on. Cut into chunky style chips approximately 7.5cm long and 1.25 cm thick. Place into boiling salted water and simmer for 7-8 minutes or until just under-cooked (*al dente*). Drain and refresh with ice-cold water to stop the cooking process. Drain well again. Place the chips in a large mixing bowl and toss with the olive oil, coating the chips in a thin layer of oil. Scatter over the Cajun seasoning and season generously with sea salt.

Sprinkle from a reasonable height, tossing to distribute the seasoning as evenly as possible.

Cover and refrigerate until ready to grill.

Barbecue Preheat the hinged sandwich rack to medium-high, or 'sizzle' temperature. Clean and lightly oil the rack. Rack up the sweet potato chips. Grill on medium-high for 6-8 minutes or until nicely charred. Turn the rack over and cook for a further 5 minutes or until cooked through and charred in spots.

To assemble the Bite Knock the chips off the rack onto a warmed oven tray. Taste for seasoning and add more salt if necessary. Serve on a beautiful plate with a bowl of Sour Cream & Chives (*see* page 190) and sprinkle with fresh coriander.

Tips Also great with limes and Roasted Garlic Mayonnaise (*see* page 178).

The natural sugar in the sweet potato caramelises beautifully in this recipe to make it one of our most popular Bites. The spicy edge is cooled perfectly with a simple dip of Sour Cream & Chives.

Charred Asparagus and Hollandaise

MAKES 48 BITES

- A hinged sandwich rack makes this recipe so much easier.
- For this very simple and delicious dish, we recommend that you buy medium-sized asparagus spears (too thin and they will fall through your grill; fat ones may be stringy and need part-peeling).

24 medium-sized asparagus spears
2 tbsp olive oil
sea salt and freshly ground pepper
Hollandaise Sauce (*see* page 180)

Slice the woody ends off the asparagus spears at a 45 degree angle and then in half, also on a 45 degree angle (cutting at an angle makes for a more elegant Bite). Cover and refrigerate until ready to grill.

You must make the Hollandaise Sauce just before grilling the asparagus, but you can prepare the ingredients in advance, i.e. separate eggs, reduce vinegar and clarify butter.

When you are ready to grill, place the asparagus in a bowl and drizzle with the olive oil, tossing to coat the spears evenly. Season well with salt and pepper.

Barbecue Preheat a barbecue sandwich rack to medium–high, or 'sizzle' temperature. Clean and lightly oil the rack. Rack up the asparagus and grill for 2–3 minutes each side, or until cooked through. A bit of charring will make them taste great.

To assemble the Bite Knock the asparagus off the rack onto a warmed oven tray. Place a plate and a bowl on a tray. Pile the charred asparagus on the plate and fill the bowl with the Hollandaise Sauce. Use your decorative imagination and throw a flower or some herbs on the tray.

Tips Can't be bothered to make your own Hollandaise? Why not try some homemade Mayonnaise (*see* page 176). We like to keep the sauce simple to allow the asparagus to speak for itself.

Spicy Jerk Plantain Chips with Pineapple, Pepper & Chilli Salsa

MAKES 65-70 BITES

• Instant marinade

• You can buy garlic and onion powders in any well-stocked Asian high street store. They are great Top Shelf ingredients.

1kg ripe, almost black plantains
2 tbsp olive oil
2 tbsp Jerk seasoning (*see* recipe below)
sea salt
Pineapple, Pepper & Chilli Salsa (*see* page 190)

Dry Rub Jerk Seasoning (fills a 450g jam jar)
1 tbsp dried thyme
1/2 tbsp allspice
1 tbsp dark brown sugar
2 tbsp black pepper
2 tbsp cayenne pepper
2 tbsp garlic powder
2 tbsp onion powder

Blend all the above ingredients together and store in an airtight jar. Another great one for your Top Shelf.

Peel the plantains, as you would a banana. Cut into chunky style chips approximately 7.5cm long and 1.25 cm thick. To achieve this, the average plantain should be cut into three and each third into 4-6 chips lengthways.

Place the chips in a large mixing bowl and toss with the olive oil, coating the chips in a thin layer of oil. Sprinkle the Jerk seasoning and salt over the chips from a reasonable height, distributing the flavouring as evenly as possible.

Cover and refrigerate until ready to grill. Use within three hours to avoid discolouring.

Barbecue Preheat a barbecue sandwich rack to medium-high, or 'sizzle' temperature. Clean and lightly oil the rack. Rack up the plantain chips. Grill for 4-5 minutes. Turn the rack over and cook for a further 5 minutes or until cooked through with a lightly charred colour. For perfect caramelisation, plantains must not be grilled too quickly. They are at their best for barbecuing when they have ripened to being almost totally black. Taste for seasoning and add more salt if necessary.

To assemble the Bite Knock the chips off the rack onto a warmed oven tray. For an exotic look, pile the chips on a banana leaf or fig leaves on a tray or plate next to the bowl of Salsa. Decorate with a few red chillies.

Tips For a really Caribbean kick, try serving with one of the many spectacularly fiery personality-packed bottled Jamaican chilli sauces available everywhere.

Plantains are exotic, very underused and fantastic on the barbecue. Like sweet potatoes, their natural sugar caramelises beautifully.

Seared Tuna Sashimi with Cucumber, Spring Onions and Wasabi Mayonnaise on Prawn Crackers

MAKES 24 BITES

- Invest in a Japanese slicer/shredder (available from most oriental supermarkets) to make the cucumber shredding a breeze. You'll find it useful for quite a few recipes in this book, and for general salad and slaw making.

300g tuna loin – the freshest you can get your
  hands on – cut into 3.5cm thick steaks
1 tbsp Szechwan peppercorns
1 tbsp vegetable oil
24 prawn crackers
vegetable oil for frying the prawn crackers
one third of a cucumber, deseeded, skin-on
2-3 spring onions
sea salt
Wasabi Mayonnaise (*see* recipe page 178)
1 large red chilli, finely diced (optional)

Ask your fishmonger to cut the tuna into 3.5cm thick steaks. Cut these tuna steaks into 3.5cm wide strips. Coarsely grind the Szechwan peppercorns in a spice grinder or pestle and mortar. Brush the tuna lightly with oil and coat in the pepper. Cover and refrigerate until ready to grill.

Deep-fry the prawn crackers following the instructions on the pack.

Finely chop the cucumber into matchstick-sized pieces, or use a mandolin. Top and tail the onion and slice, using a sharp knife, very finely on a diagonal.

Season the tuna with salt before grilling

Barbecue Preheat the barbecue grill to high. It must be smoking hot with intense heat. Clean and lightly oil the rack. Sear the tuna for 40-60 seconds on all sides, rolling the strip of tuna with tongs or a fish slice to char each side. Do not overcook: tuna is at its best blue to rare.

To assemble the Bite Slice the tuna finely. Place your prawn crackers on a tray or chopping board. Top with cucumber and spring onion. Place the tuna slice on top, trying to twist some shape into it. Using a teaspoon or a piping bag, dollop a small amount of Wasabi Mayonnaise on top of the tuna and sprinkle with the finely diced chilli. Arrange on a funky plate.

Tips Instead of prawn crackers, try wonton wrappers, sliced into quarters, i.e triangles, and deep-fried.

A little time consuming to put together, but the entertaining, end result is well worth the effort.

Tiger Prawns Grilled with Lemon, Garlic and Herbs served with Saffron Aioli

MAKES 30 BITES

- 3 hour marinade

- If you can't get fresh or if you want to save yourself money, buy peeled raw frozen tiger prawns for this one. Oriental supermarkets sell them in big bags – a great product. At Blistering, for perfect even grilling, we always barbecue prawns on stainless steel skewers – an essential tool for the barbecue. Invest in some now.
- Often, frozen prawns are size-graded according to how many there are in a kilogram. We find that the so-called '20/30's (i.e. 20-30 to the kilogram) are ideal for Bites. For more information on prawns, *see* page 126 in Fish and Shellfish.

30 raw peeled tiger prawns, de-veined
4 x 30cm metal skewers, or equivalent

For the marinade
6 cloves garlic, finely chopped
fine zest of three lemons
3 tbsp chopped fresh tarragon
2 tbsp chopped fresh dill
2 tbsp olive oil

sea salt and freshly ground pepper
juice of 2 lemons, or to taste
Saffron Aioli (*see* page177)

Defrost the prawns. Drain them in a colander.

For the marinade Mix the chopped garlic with the lemon zest (reserve the juice for later), tarragon, dill and olive oil in a bowl. Toss in the prawns and coat well with the marinade mix.

Spike onto stainless steel skewers, skewering firstly through the thick head–end and then through the tail of each prawn. Lining up the prawns in this way makes for even cooking on the barbecue.

Cover and marinate in the fridge for up to 3 hours.

Barbecue Preheat the barbecue grill to high. Clean and lightly oil the rack. Season the prawns with salt and pepper. Place the skewers on the grill and cook for 1–2 minutes on each side or until nearly cooked through. Grill time will vary according to the size of the prawns. Prawns will continue to cook for a couple of minutes after you remove them from the barbecue. Be careful not to overcook them, as you'll lose that delicious juiciness as they begin to toughen up.

To assemble the Bite Using a fork or your fingers, remove the prawns from the skewer a few at a time. If you try to remove them all with one push from the top of the skewer, you will damage some of them. Pile in a bowl and squeeze over the lemon juice. Serve with a bowl of Saffron Aioli.

Tips Never marinate prawns with lemon juice. The acid 'cooks' the flesh before it gets a chance to hit the barbecue grill.

Prawns are nature's perfect package for barbecuing.

Griddled Squid with Blistering Sweet Chilli Sauce

MAKES 24 BITES

• 3 hour to overnight marinade

• If spankingly fresh squid isn't available, look out for frozen cleaned squid tubes.

350g large squid tubes (defrosted, if using frozen)

For the marinade
4 tbsp Blistering Sweet Chilli Sauce (*see* page 187)
1 thumb fresh ginger, peeled and finely chopped
5 cloves garlic, peeled and finely chopped
1 tbsp vegetable oil

fine sea salt and freshly ground pepper
juice of 2 small limes, or to taste
fresh coriander, chopped, or to taste

To prepare the squid Slice down one side of the squid tube, so that it opens out flat on a chopping board. If the fishmonger hasn't done so already, discard the transparent plastic-like quill and the guts and wash the squid under cold running water. Pat dry with paper towels. Using a sharp cook's knife, score the inner, softer side of the opened tube to make a neat diamond pattern. Score no further than halfway through the flesh. Cut the scored squid into rectangles measuring approximately 3.75 x 2.5 cm.

Mix together the marinade ingredients. In a large bowl, toss the squid in the marinade.

Spike the squid rectangles widthways onto stainless steel skewers, like sails on a child's toy, the diamond pattern facing outwards. Once skewered, pour any excess marinade back over the squid.

Cover and marinate in the fridge for at least three hours or preferably overnight

Barbecue Squid must be cooked quickly: if cooked slowly, it becomes tough and rubbery. Squid is a notorious sticker, so clean and lightly oil the rack. Preheat the sandwich rack to high or 'searing' temperature. Season the squid with salt and pepper. Place the skewers on the rack and cook for 1-1^1/$_2$ minutes on either side, or until just opaque.

To assemble the Bite Using a fork or your fingers, slide the squid off the skewers into a mixing bowl. Working quickly, toss with the lime juice and fresh coriander. Pile the squid in a bowl and serve.

Tips At Blistering, we remove the grill from the barbecue and lie the skewers across the barbecue trough to bypass the problem of sticking and to bring the squid flesh as close to the heat as possible.

To generate enormous heat, to save your time skewering and to add a touch of drama to the party, place a wok directly on the hot coals and allow to heat until smoking. Throw in the marinated squid with a 'chssssh' and toss for 1^1/$_2$-2 minutes, or until cooked through.

When we first started using squid for Bites, we didn't think it would be that popular. So, when it first appeared on our menu, we were pleasantly surprised to discover that the guests couldn't get enough of it.

Rare Charred Pepper Steak Sandwiches with Grainy Mustard Mayonnaise, Watercress and 'Sunblush' Tomato Pesto
MAKES 24 BITES

• We find that thin ciabatta sticks are ideal for the purpose.

350g sirloin steak, cut about 2.5 cm thick
1 tbsp vegetable oil
fine sea salt and freshly ground pepper
3 x part-baked ciabatta sticks or 1 long thin part-baked baguette
'Sunblush' Tomato Pesto (*see* page 192)
2 tbsp mayonnaise blended with 1tbsp grainy mustard
150g watercress, washed
24 cocktail sticks

Trim the sirloin free of fat and gristle and cut lengthways into 2 strips. Brush lightly with vegetable oil. Season well with salt and pepper.

Slice the bread in half, lengthways.

Barbecue Preheat the barbecue grill to medium-high, or 'sizzle' temperature. Clean and lightly oil the rack. For a medium-rare steak, grill for 1$^{1}/_{2}$-2 minutes on each of the four sides or until cooked as desired. If you have bought thinner-cut steaks off the supermarket shelf, then just grill the strips of steak on each of the 2 sides for approximately 3 minutes, or until cooked as desired. It is very important that you allow the steak to rest for a few minutes after cooking and before slicing. This allows the sinews to relax so that the steak won't be tough and makes for a rosier, less fleshy steak that doesn't lose its juices when cut.

To assemble the Bite Toast the bread lengths on a medium heat until golden-brown on both sides. Spread the top half of the bread with 'Sunblush' Tomato Pesto and the bottom with the grainy mustard mayonnaise. Slice your steak thinly, on an angle, to suit the size of your bread. Place the steak on the bottom half of the sandwich, followed by sprigs of watercress. Finish with the top half of the loaf.

Place the loaf/loaves on a chopping board and trim off the ends. Starting 2 cm from the cut end, push cocktail skewers into each long sandwich 4 cm apart all the way down the loaf. Using a sharp bread knife, slice between each skewer at a 45 degree angle.

Tips These and many other sandwiches off the grill are great as larger handheld snacks, as well as Bites.

This is a mini version of a favourite. You can't beat a well-made sandwich. Try Bacon and Caesar or Jerk Pork fillet with Mango Salsa and Crunchy Salad. Let your imagination carry you away.

Selection of Blistering Cocktail Sausages served with Dips

- At Blistering we use award-winning Villagers Fine Sausages (*see* Suppliers' appendix, page 215) for both cocktail and full-size sausages. They are handmade with fine, imaginative ingredients and no preservatives. With his expertise in sausage-making, the owner, Ron, has even appeared on BBC's *The Generation Game*.
- Some of our favourite flavours include Toulouse, Spicy Sicilian, Chorizo and Lamb & Mint. We find that the sausages with a higher fat content are juicier for barbecuing.
- A sandwich rack is essential for cooking cocktail sausages. When the fat starts dripping and the flames start licking, you want to be able to recover and turn your sausages in a hurry.

De-link the sausages. Line up on the sandwich rack.

Barbecue Preheat the barbecue grill or hinged sandwich rack to medium-high or 'sizzle' temperature. Clean and lightly oil the rack. Grill the sausages at a sufficient distance above the coals to ensure that the flames caused by the dripping oil do not reach the sausages. Grill for 3-4 minutes on each side, or until cooked through to the middle.

To assemble the Bite Place each sausage type in a separate bowl and serve with any of the dips and sauces suggested on pages 176-196.

Tips For straight pork or Cumberland sausages, try tossing the hot barbecued sausages in honey and toasted sesame seeds.

If anyone knows about barbecuing sausages, we do.

Japanese Chicken with Sake Mustard Marinade served with Sweet Soy & Pickled Ginger Dip

MAKES 32-40 BITES

• **3 hour to overnight marinade**

4 x 150g chicken breasts, boneless and skinless
3 x 30cm metal skewers, or equivalent

For the marinade
2 tbsp vegetable oil
2 tsp white mustard seeds
2 tsp black mustard seeds
6 tbsp Sake
2 tbsp palm sugar
2 tsp wasabi paste
1 tbsp mild Yellow Hot Dog Mustard
1 tsp turmeric
1tsp sesame oil

fine sea salt and freshly ground pepper
juice of 1 lemon
Sweet Soy & Pickled Ginger Dip (*see* page 185)

Heat the vegetable oil in a saucepan. Pour the mustard seeds into the hot oil, turn the heat right down and put a lid on immediately. Shake the pan vigorously to prevent the seeds from burning, cooking them until they pop and give off a toasted nutty aroma (about 20-30 seconds).

Pour the Sake carefully into the hot saucepan. Beware – the Sake may well ignite as the alcohol hits the hot oil, so watch your eyebrows. Add the sugar and reduce the pan contents by one third. Remove from the heat. Add the wasabi, mustard, turmeric and sesame oil. Allow to cool in a roomy bowl.

Cut each chicken breast in half lengthways. Cut each half breast into 4 or 5 even-sized pieces. Place the chicken pieces in the marinade. Stir with a spoon coating each piece well.

Thread the chicken onto stainless steel skewers. Place on a plate or tray. Once skewered, pour any excess marinade back over the chicken.

Cover and refrigerate, marinating for at least 3 hours, or preferably overnight. Having a low-fat content, chicken breast is prone to sticking to a barbecue. At Blistering, to avoid sticking, we rub down the hot sandwich racks with an old pure cotton tea towel dabbed with vegetable oil. You could try this using protective mits or, alternatively, lightly brush the chicken skewers with vegetable oil.

Barbecue Preheat the barbecue sandwich racks to medium-high. Clean and lightly oil the rack. Season the skewers with salt and pepper. Place the skewers on the rack and cook for 3-4 minutes on each side, or until cooked through. Be careful not to overcook the breasts, as they become dry and unappealing.

To assemble the Bite Using a fork or your fingers, remove the chicken pieces from the skewer a few at a time into a mixing bowl. If you try to remove them all with one push from the top of the skewer, you will damage some of them. Adjust the seasoning to taste and toss with lemon juice. Transfer the chicken pieces to a serving bowl and serve with Sweet Soy & Pickled Ginger dip and a bundle of cocktail sticks or small bamboo skewers.

Tips For authenticity, serve with a shot glass of warmed Sake.

Wasabi paste needn't just be a green fiery dollop next to your sushi: it's a terrific punchy marinade ingredient. Get some for your Top Shelf.

Green Thai Chicken with Fresh Thai Basil and Coconut Curry Dipping Sauce

MAKES 32-40 BITES

- 3 hour to overnight marinade

- It's well worth your while taking a trip to your nearest oriental food stores to stock up cheaply on the following marinade ingredients. They are all great Top Shelf ingredients with long shelf lives. You don't really need to add the Thai green curry paste, but we do find that it gives that extra spice and oomph.

4 x 150g chicken breasts, boneless and skinless
3 x 30cm metal skewers, or equivalent

For the marinade
2 tbsp vegetable oil
4 cloves garlic, finely chopped
1 thumb ginger, peeled and finely chopped
4 tsp Thai green curry paste, optional
4 tsp fish sauce (nam pla)
4 lime leaves
4 tbsp palm sugar
2 tsp ground dried shrimp
2 tbsp water
6 tbsp coconut milk
2 tsp Thai basil, roughly chopped (optional)
2 tbsp fresh coriander stalks and leaves, roughly chopped

sea salt and freshly ground pepper
juice of 2 small limes, or to taste
Coconut Curry Dipping Sauce (*see* page 186)

Heat the oil in a heavy-bottomed stainless steel pan. Fry the garlic and ginger until golden brown. Turn the heat down low and, stirring, add the curry paste, fish sauce, lime leaves, palm sugar, dried shrimp and water. Cook for a couple of minutes to blend the flavours. Pour in the coconut milk, whisking as you do so. Turn off the heat. Let it cool down. When cool, add the herbs.

Follow the cutting, marinating, skewering and refrigeration steps from the preceding Japanese Chicken recipe.

Barbecue *See* preceding Japanese Chicken recipe for barbecuing instructions.

To assemble the Bite Using a fork or your fingers, remove the chicken pieces from the skewer a few at a time into a mixing bowl. If you try to remove them all with one push from the top of the skewer, you will damage some of them. Adjust the seasoning to taste and toss with lime juice. Transfer the chicken pieces to a serving bowl and serve with Coconut Curry Dipping Sauce.

Tips For a super-quick version, just blend the Thai curry paste with the coconut milk – and you have an authentic-tasting marinade in seconds.

Get down to your nearest oriental food store to stock up your Top Shelf.

Chicken Shish Taouk Marinated in Lemon, Coriander and Moroccan Spices with Pomegranate Molasses & Mint Dipping Sauce   MAKES 32-40 BITES

• 3 hour to overnight marinade

4 x 150g chicken breasts, boneless and skinless
3 x 30cm metal skewers, or equivalent

For the marinade
1/2 medium onion, roughly chopped
2 cloves garlic, peeled and chopped
3 tbsp vegetable oil
zest of 1 lemon
1 tsp ground cumin
1/2 tsp ground coriander seeds
1/2 tsp ground cinnamon
1/4 tsp grated nutmeg
scant 1/4 tsp ground cloves
   (warning – do not overdo the cloves!)
1 tsp paprika
1/2 tsp cayenne pepper
1/2 tsp sumac
1 tbsp soft brown sugar
2 tbsp fresh coriander
2 tbsp fresh flat leaf parsley

sea salt and freshly ground pepper
Pomegranate Molasses & Mint Dipping Sauce
   (see page 195)

Pulse the onion and garlic in a blender until almost smooth, but not puréed. Heat the oil in a heavy-bottomed stainless steel pan and cook the onion and garlic mix on a medium heat, stirring continuously for 2-3 minutes.

Add the lemon zest, cumin, coriander, cinnamon, nutmeg, cloves, paprika and cayenne and cook for 5 minutes on a low heat to really bring out the flavours. Allow to cool slightly before adding the remaining marinade ingredients.

Follow the cutting, marinating, skewering and refrigeration steps from the Japanese Chicken recipe (*see* page 40).

Barbecue *See* Japanese Chicken recipe for barbecuing instructions.

To assemble the Bite Using a fork or your fingers, remove the chicken pieces from the skewer a few at a time into a mixing bowl. Adjust the seasoning to taste. Transfer the chicken pieces to a serving bowl and serve with Pomegranate Molasses & Mint Dipping Sauce.

Tips Try this one with Minted Yoghurt and some grilled flat breads for a tapas plate.

This is a terrific Middle Eastern spice combination not only for chicken, but for all meats and firm fish. Make up a jar and keep it in your fridge.

Baby Back Ribs in Chinese Sticky Sweet & Sour Sauce

MAKES ABOUT 24 BABY RIBS

• 3 hour to overnight marinade

• You can use this recipe for a full-size rack of ribs also.

2kg baby back ribs

For the cooking liquor
200ml soy sauce
100g sugar
2 tbsp Chinese five spice
6 star anise
5 tsp dried chilli flakes (or to taste for 'Hot and Sour')
2 onions, peeled and chopped in half
2 thumbs fresh ginger, peeled and roughly chopped

For the marinade
100ml tomato ketchup
30ml sweet soy sauce (or Ketjap Manis)
30ml rice vinegar
20g brown sugar
1tsp dried chilli flakes (optional – but necessary if you want it 'Hot and Sour')

Place the rack of ribs in a large pan and cover with cold water. Add all the cooking liquor ingredients. Bring to the boil and skim off the froth. Simmer for 35-40 minutes, skimming as the froth or scum develops. Take the pan off the heat and allow the ribs to cool in the liquor. Once cool, strain through a colander.

Combine the marinade ingredients. Knock the cooking liquor ingredients off the ribs. Place the ribs in a bowl and coat thoroughly with the marinade. Cover and refrigerate for 3 hours, or preferably overnight.

Before barbecuing Give the ribs enough time out of the fridge to lose their chill.

Barbecue Preheat the barbecue grill to medium, or 'cook' temperature. Clean and lightly oil the rack. The ribs are already cooked, so in this barbecuing process, you are caramelising the marinade, and heating the meat through to the middle, while retaining the moisture. Grill the ribs for 10 minutes, basting regularly with excess marinade, so that the ribs turn out sticky, as billed.

To assemble the Bite Place the ribs on a chopping board. Hold a rack of ribs standing upright like a parade of soldiers. Using a sharp heavy knife, cut down between the ribs leaving an even amount of meat on either side. Pile in a bowl and serve immediately.

Tips This is a messy one, so set up a few lemon finger bowls with plenty of napkins. If you have Asian Top Shelf Sauce (*see* page 188) to hand, you may choose to use this instead of the marinade.

Not the most elegant of Bites, but there is something primeval about the combination of fire and eating barbecued meat off the bone.

Indonesian Grilled Lamb Marinated with Sweet Soy, Star Anise, Tamarind and Palm Sugar served with Coriander & Ginger Pesto

MAKES ABOUT 48 BITES

• 3 hour to overnight marinade

• This is not a cut of meat to serve rare, because it ends up chewy. Medium is great.

3 whole lamb neck fillets (about 1.2kg)

1 tbsp vegetable oil
2 cloves garlic, finely chopped
2 tbsp Pernod
1/2 tsp dried chilli flakes, or to taste
4 star anise
1/2 tbsp palm sugar
2 tbsp water
2 tbsp sweet soy sauce
2 tsp tamarind paste

sea salt and freshly ground black pepper
Coriander & Ginger Pesto (*see* page 187)

Trim the lamb neck fillet free of sinew and excess fat. Slice lengthways into 1.5cm wide strips.

Heat the oil in a heavy-bottomed stainless steel pan and cook the garlic until golden brown. Taking great care, pour the Pernod into the hot saucepan. Beware – the Pernod may well spit and ignite as the alcohol hits the hot oil, so watch your hands and eyebrows. Turn the heat down to medium and add the chilli flakes, star anise, palm sugar and water, stirring until the sugar is dissolved. Take off the heat and add the sweet soy sauce and tamarind paste. Allow to cool. Put the lamb neck and the cooled marinade in a strong plastic bag, massage the bag to distribute the marinade over all the surfaces of the meat. Refrigerate for at least 3 hours, or preferably overnight.

Before barbecuing Give the lamb enough time out of the fridge to lose its chill. Season with salt and pepper to taste.

Barbecue Preheat the barbecue grill to medium-high, or 'sizzle' temperature. Clean and lightly oil the rack. Place the meat strips on the grill and sear on all sides. Move to a medium heat and continue to grill, basting with a little of the marinade liquid on all sides to stop it from drying out. Grill on one side for 4-5 minutes. Turn and cook for a further 4-5 minutes on the other side, or until cooked as desired.

It is very important that you allow the lamb to rest for 3-4 minutes before slicing. This allows the sinews to relax and so prevents the meat from becoming chewy and losing its juices.

To assemble the Bite Carve the lamb into bite-size pieces. Pile on a small plate with some small bamboo skewers or cocktail sticks. Accompany with a small bowl of Coriander & Ginger Pesto.

Tips Try lamb with the Shish Taouk (*see* page 43) marinade. The sweetness of the lamb meets the mellowness of Middle Eastern spices beautifully.

With its delicious sweetish flavour and its good fat content, neck of lamb lends itself beautifully to barbecuing.

SNACKS, WRAPS AND BURGERS

Original Red Leb Chicken Wrap

MAKES 6 SNACKS

- 3 hour to overnight marinade

- The following recipes use large (i.e. 24cm) tortillas. If using smaller ones you will need to adjust the quantities and fill the wraps appropriately. The rolling method is always the same. You need to find a suitable sauce to use as the wrapping 'glue', then fill the wrap with a combination of hot and cold ingredients, and you're away.
- The ingredients list may seem long, but this is not a complicated process. It's just a matter of having a well-stocked Top Shelf. Make up a jar of paste, whack it in the fridge and barbecue your way through June, July and August.
- The grated fresh beetroot gives the marinade a great colour.

4-5 x 150g chicken breasts, no skin, no bone
3 x 30cm metal skewers or equivalent

For the Red Leb Marinade (makes about 750g)
2 onions, peeled and roughly chopped
8 cloves garlic, skinned and roughly chopped
2 thumbs fresh ginger, peeled and roughly chopped
3 tbsp coriander seeds
3 tbsp cumin seeds
1 tbsp fennel seeds
8 cardamom pods
2 cinnamon sticks
10 cloves
8 tbsp vegetable oil
2 tbsp black mustard seeds
1 tsp freshly ground black pepper
1 tbsp pomegranate powder (optional)
$1/4$ tsp freshly ground nutmeg
2 tsp red chilli flakes
1 large raw beetroot, peeled and freshly grated

For grilling and assembling the wraps
2 tbsp Red Leb marinade (*see* above)
vegetable oil for brushing

fine sea salt
juice of 1 lemon
6 large (24cm) flour tortillas or Lebanese flatbreads
6 level tbsp Hummus (*see* page 188)
175g carrot, match-sticked or grated
175g red cabbage, finely shredded
5-6 spring onions, finely sliced
1 bunch fresh coriander, chopped
Blistering Sweet Chilli Sauce (*see* page 188), to taste
4 tbsp natural yoghurt, preferably strained Greek

For the marinade Place the onions, garlic and ginger in a blender and pulse to a purée. Heat a heavy-bottomed saucepan or skillet, which has a lid. Pour in coriander, cumin, fennel, cardamom, cinnamon and cloves. Toast in the hot pan, shaking to prevent catching until the spices begin to smell aromatic. Remove from the pan and grind in a spice grinder or pestle and mortar. Heat the oil in the same pan and fry the mustard seeds. Place on the lid and, shaking the pan over the heat to prevent catching, fry for approximately 30 seconds or until aromatic and toasted. Turn down the heat to low-medium and add the onion, garlic and ginger mixture. Cook gently for 4–5 minutes stirring regularly until the water has evaporated, but the mix has not browned. Add all the ingredients, with the exception of the beetroot, and continue to cook slowly for a further 3 minutes to fuse the flavours. Add the beetroot with 100ml water and cook for 3 minutes. Transfer to a tray to chill quickly. Spoon into a sterilised jar and refrigerate.

To marinate the chicken Cut the chicken into 2.5 cm dice and place in a bowl with 2 tablespoons of Red Leb marinade.

Using disposable gloves, mix well. Thread onto metal skewers, cover and refrigerate overnight or for at least 3 hours.

Before barbecuing Give the chicken enough time out of the fridge to lose its chill. Brush lightly with oil, season with salt as desired. Before you begin barbecuing, have all your wrap ingredients lined up and ready to go.

Barbecue Preheat the grill to medium-high or 'sizzle' temperature. Clean and lightly oil the rack. Grill the skewers for a total of 3-5 minutes on each side, or until cooked through, turning regularly to prevent burning. Remove to a warmed tray. Squeeze over the lemon juice. Cover and leave to rest for 3-4 minutes while you organise yourself for assembling the wraps. If using Lebanese breads, warm the breads on the barbecue to make them more flexible.

To assemble the Wraps Place your wraps flat on a work surface. Spread hummus over the top half of the wrap. When you roll the wraps, this will act as a 'glue'. Divide the carrots, cabbage, spring onions and coriander between the wraps and arrange in a horizontal strip about a third of the way up the wrap, below the hummus line. Top with the hot pieces of chicken, spoon over the Blistering Sweet Chilli Sauce and yoghurt. Roll tightly like a cigar, sealing with the hummus. Place back on the barbecue, with the sealed edge downwards first and toast briefly all over. Slice on a diagonal and serve.

Tips Beware this marinade: it will stain anything that gets in its way!

A nostalgic dish for us. When we first met back in the early '90's, we were serving 2,000 of these a day on the award-winning Red Leb stall at Glastonbury Festival. We're still serving them now, but to a different crowd.

Mexican Beef Fajitas with Refried Beans, Guacamole, Sour Cream and Coriander

MAKES 6 SNACKS

- 3 hour plus or overnight marinade

- Make the refried beans and marinate your meat a day ahead. You could always buy in the refried beans and the guacamole – there are some splendid ones knocking around on the shelves these days – but homemade is best of course.
- Chipotle chillies have a great, unique and very spicy taste, but if you can't get hold of them, replace them with your normal chillies.

3 x 225g sirloin steaks

For the Mexican Marinade
2 tsp cumin seeds
1 or 2 tinned chipotle chillies (or other available), or to taste, finely chopped
4 cloves garlic, finely chopped
$1/4$ tsp freshly ground pepper
$1^1/2$ tbsp olive oil

To grill the meat and assemble the Fajitas
olive oil for brushing
fine sea salt
6 large (24cm) flour tortillas or equivalent
1 recipe quantity Refried Beans (see page 196)
1 red pepper, finely sliced
6 spring onions, finely sliced
3 tbsp chopped coriander
6 tbsp Guacamole (see page 190 – one recipe quantity is more than enough)
142ml tub soured cream

To marinate the meat Toast the cumin seeds in a dry skillet or frying pan. Grind in a spice grinder or pestle and mortar. Mix in a bowl with the other marinade ingredients. Using disposable gloves, rub the steaks with the marinade and massage it all over the meat. Cover or bag tightly and refrigerate overnight or for at least 3 hours.

Before barbecuing Give the steak enough time out of the fridge to lose its chill. Brush lightly with oil and season with salt as desired. Before you begin barbecuing, have all your fajita ingredients lined up and ready to go.

Barbecue Preheat the grill to medium-high or 'sizzle' temperature. Clean and lightly oil the rack. Place the steaks on the grill and seal for 1–2 minutes on each side. Grill for a further 1–3 minutes on each side or until cooked as desired. Grill times vary widely, depending on the thickness of the cut.

Remove the steaks to a warmed tray. Cover and leave to rest for 3–4 minutes while you organise yourself for assembling the wraps.

If using Lebanese breads, warm the breads on the barbecue to make them more flexible. Warm the refried beans.

To assemble the Wraps Place your wraps flat on a work surface. Spread refried beans over the top half of the wrap. When you roll the wraps, this will act as a 'glue'.

Wrapping is a great handheld way of enjoying barbecued food, so here's another one – the original wrap, you could say.

Divide the red pepper, spring onions and coriander between the wraps and arrange in a horizontal strip about a third of the way up each wrap. Slice the warm barbecued steak into thin strips and lay them on top of the vegetables. Dollop the guacamole and the sour cream onto the vegetables. Roll like a cigar, sealing with the refried beans. Place back on the barbecue, with the sealed edge downwards and toast briefly all over. Slice on a diagonal and serve.

Tips This recipe is very versatile and is suitable for any meat, from pork tenderloin to chicken breast. Also delicious with prawns, if you keep the marinating process down to no more that 2 hours.

Hoi Sin Duck Wrap
with Cucumber and Spring Onion

MAKES 6 SNACKS

• 3 hour plus or overnight marinade

5-6 female or small duck breasts
 (approximately 750g total weight)

For the marinade
1 thumb fresh ginger, finely chopped
4 cloves garlic, finely chopped
$1/4$ tsp chilli flakes
4 tbsp sweet soy sauce (or Indonesian Ketjap Manis)
2 tsp sugar
1 level tbsp Chinese five spice powder

For grilling and assembling the Wraps
vegetable oil for brushing the meat
$2^{1}/_{2}$ tbsp Hoi Sin sauce
$2^{1}/_{2}$ tbsp plum sauce
1 medium cucumber
6 large (24cm) flour tortillas, or equivalent
10 spring onions, cut on the diagonal
75g pink pickled ginger, drained

To prepare the duck Place the duck breasts skin side down on the chopping board. Run your fingers along between the fatty skin and the meat to begin to separate the two.

Keeping the breasts skin side down, trim the loose fat off to around 5mm from the edges of the meat on each side and at the top and the bottom of each breast. Do not trim off any of the meat. Turn the breast skin-side up and score the fat at 1cm intervals, criss-crossed on a diagonal, giving a diamond harlequin pattern.

To marinate the duck Combine the marinade ingredients in a mixing bowl. Place the prepared duck breasts in the bowl, making sure that all breasts are well covered with the marinade. Transfer the duck and any excess marinade to a strong plastic bag. Tie the top tightly and give it a good massage. Refrigerate overnight or for at least 3 hours.

Before barbecuing Give the duck enough time out of the fridge to lose its chill. Brush lightly with oil. Have all your wrap ingredients lined up and ready to go. Mix the Hoi Sin and plum sauces in a bowl. Cut the cucumber into two and quarter each half lengthways.

In this way you can slice out the seeds easily. Then slice the firm flesh into long thin strips.

Barbecue Duck is at its most tender when cooked pink, so be careful not to overcook it. Preheat the barbecue to medium. Clean and lightly oil the rack. The following times apply to female duck breasts; larger male breasts take longer. For a pink-medium result, place the duck breasts skin-side down on the barbecue grill or sandwich rack. Grill for 4-5 minutes to produce a crispy skin before turning. Grill on the flesh side for a further 4-5 minutes. Place on a warm plate or tray, cover with foil (leaving a gap to allow steam to escape) and let the duck rest for at least 5 minutes before carving.

To assemble the wraps Place your wraps flat on a work surface. Spread the Hoi Sin and plum sauce mix over the top half of the wrap. When you roll the wraps, this will act as a 'glue'. Divide all the cold ingredients between the wraps, arranging them in horizontal strips about a third of the way up each of the wraps. Slice the warm duck breasts thinly and lay them on top of the other ingredients. Roll tightly like a cigar, sealing with the sauce. Place back on the barbecue with the sealed edge downwards and toast briefly all over. Slice on the diagonal and serve.

This is our quick and more succulent take on the classic Peking Crispy Duck Pancake.

Japanese Teriyaki Prawn Wrap with Wasabi Mayonnaise

MAKES 6 SNACKS

- Maximum 2 hour marinade

- This is where a Japanese mandolin comes in very handy – an indispensable piece of equipment, which enables you to produce perfectly match-sticked vegetables before you can say 'Rick Stein'.
- For more information on prawns, *see* page 126.

30 raw peeled tiger prawns, de-veined
4 x 30cm metal skewers, or equivalent

For the marinade
3 tbsp teriyaki sauce
1 tbsp vegetable oil
2 tsp soft brown sugar
1 thumb ginger, finely chopped

For grilling
juice of one lime

Also for the sandwich
1 tbsp sesame seeds
175g kohlrabi (or, if unavailable, carrot), matchsticked, or finely shredded on a Japanese mandolin
8 radishes, finely sliced (optional)
$1/2$ yellow pepper, finely sliced
$1/2$ red pepper, finely sliced
4-5 spring onions, finely sliced on the bias
4 tbsp chopped fresh coriander
2 tbsp teriyaki sauce
1 tbsp sesame oil
6 large (24cm) flour tortillas, or equivalent
2 generous tbsp Wasabi Mayonnaise (*see* page 178)

To marinate the prawns Combine the marinade ingredients in a bowl. Dry the prawns thoroughly on kitchen paper and toss in the marinade, coating them well. Marinate for no more than 2 hours. Thread onto stainless steel skewers, skewering firstly through the thick head-end and then through the tail of each prawn. For even grilling, don't pack them too tightly on the skewer.

Before barbecuing Give the prawns enough time out of the fridge to lose their chill. Prepare the other wrap ingredients. Toast the sesame seeds in a dry skillet or frying pan. Be careful, as they will pop and fly out of the pan. Having a high oil content, they also burn easily, so hold a lid loosely over the pan and shake the pan as the seeds toast. Place the prepared kohlrabi, radishes (if using), peppers, spring onions and coriander in a bowl and toss with the teriyaki sauce, toasted sesame seeds and sesame oil.

Barbecue Preheat the grill to medium-high or 'sizzle' temperature. Clean and lightly oil the rack. Grill the prawn skewers for 2-3 minutes on each side until the prawns are firm and opaque, but not charred and shrinking. Be very careful, as prawns are incredibly devalued by over-cooking. They will continue to cook for a couple of minutes after you remove them from the barbecue.

A delicious crunch with clean oriental flavours and a kick of wasabi.

To assemble the wraps Using a fork, push the prawns off the skewers into a bowl, a couple at a time. Sprinkle with the fresh lime juice and more seasoning if required. Place your wraps flat on a work surface. Dividing it equally between the 6 wraps, spread the Wasabi mayonnaise over the top half of the wrap. When you roll the wraps, this will act as a 'glue'. Divide all the remaining ingredients between the wraps, arranging them in a horizontal strip about a third of the way up each of the wraps. Leave any excess teriyaki and sesame dressing behind in the bowl – you don't want the wrap to be soggy. Roll tightly like a cigar, sealing with the mayonnaise. Place back on the barbecue, with the sealed edge downwards and toast briefly all over. Slice on the diagonal and serve.

Tips If you know and love your wasabi, boost the heat of this wrap by spreading a tiny dollop of the pure green paste across the width of the wrap before filling it... but be careful!

Lamb Shwarma Kebab with Spinach, Red Onion, Peppers, Blistering Sweet Chilli Sauce, Garlic Yoghurt Sauce and Pickled Green Chillies   MAKES 6 SNACKS

• 3 hour to overnight marinade

• Pomegranate molasses are one of our favourite Top Shelf ingredients (see Suppliers appendix, page 215).

700g trimmed neck fillet

For the marinade
3 tsp coriander seeds
3 tsp cumin seeds
2 tsp mild paprika
1½ tbsp pomegranate molasses
¼ tsp freshly ground black pepper
1½ tbsp olive oil

For grilling the lamb
fine sea salt

To assemble the Kebabs
150g white cabbage, finely sliced
75g baby spinach leaves
½ red onion, finely sliced
Juice of 1 lemon
6 pitta breads
3 medium-sized tomatoes, sliced into rounds
8 pickled green chillies, or to taste

Garlic Yoghurt Sauce (see page 181)
Blistering Sweet Chilli Sauce (see page 187)

To marinate the meat Toast the coriander and cumin seeds over the heat in a dry skillet or frying pan. Grind in a spice grinder or pestle and mortar. Mix in a bowl with the other marinade ingredients. Using disposable gloves, rub the lamb all over with the marinade. Cover and refrigerate overnight or for at least 3 hours.

To grill the lamb Before barbecuing, give the lamb enough time out of the fridge to lose its chill. This cut of lamb has a relatively high fat and weak sinew content, so needs slow cooking. Season the lamb well with salt. Before you begin barbecuing, have all your kebab ingredients lined up and ready to go.

Barbecue Preheat the grill to medium-high or 'sizzle' temperature. Clean and lightly oil the rack. A clean grill is particularly important for this recipe, as the pomegranate molasses can make the lamb prone to sticking. Place the lamb on the grill and seal on all sides. This should take about 2-3 minutes. Move to a medium heat and cook for a further 12-15 minutes, or until cooked through, turning every 3 minutes or so.

Remove the lamb to a warmed tray. Cover and leave to rest for 3-4 minutes while you organise yourself to assemble the kebabs.

To assemble the kebabs Toss the cabbage, spinach and red onion with the lemon juice and season to taste. Slice the lamb thinly on the diagonal, across the grain of the meat, to give doner-kebab-like strips. Warm the pitta breads on the barbecue for a minute on each side until they puff up and are easy to split. Don't toast them, as they will become inflexible. Split the bread down one side. Divide the dressed cabbage and spinach mix between the pittas and top with the tomato and chilli, finishing with the Garlic Yoghurt Sauce and the Blistering Sweet Chilli Sauce.

Tips We like to serve these kebabs with the extra sauce option of Mint Mojo (*see* page 190).

The most popular kebab in the world. How about trying this top kebab when you are relatively sober?

Chorizo Sausage, Tomato and Rocket Sandwich with Rocket Pesto and Roast Garlic Mayonnaise

MAKES 6 SANDWICHES

- We just had to include a sausage sandwich. Though we are more than capable of banging out a great Cumberland Sausage Sandwich with ketchup, this is our hands-down favourite.
- You will have to hunt down the softer 'cooking' or 'frying' chorizo sausage for this recipe. Don't buy the firm slicing chorizo: it's too hard (*see* Villagers Fine Sausages, in the supplier appendix). Both of the sauces we suggest using here are very versatile and will keep well in the fridge for a few days.

1kg soft frying chorizo sausage, de-linked
6 ciabatta rolls
Roast Garlic Mayonnaise (*see* page 178)
Rocket Pesto (*see* page 182)
2 bunches rocket, washed and spun
2 tomatoes, sliced into rounds

Before barbecuing, give the sausages enough time out of the fridge to lose their chill. Also assemble the salad ingredients, so that you can assemble your sandwich easily while the sausages are still hot.

Barbecue Preheat the grill to medium-high or 'sizzle' temperature. Clean and lightly oil the rack. Grill the sausages turning every couple of minutes for a total of 6–8 minutes or until cooked through. Grill time will vary depending on the thickness of the sausages. Remove the sausages from the grill onto a chopping board.

To assemble the sandwich Slice open the rolls and toast lightly on the barbecue. Spread Roast Garlic Mayonnaise generously on one cut side and Rocket Pesto on the other. Scrunch up a handful of rocket and place on the base, followed by slices of tomato. You don't want the sausages to dry out or to lose any juices, so slice the hot chorizo lengthways in two just before placing it in the sandwich on top of the tomato. Replace the tops and serve immediately while the chorizo is still hot.

This is our hands-down favourite sausage sandwich.

Griddled Classic Prawn Cocktail Granary Sandwich with Marie Rose Sauce, Lemon, Cos and Watercress

MAKES 6 SANDWICHES

• 2 hour to overnight marinade

• Prawn cocktail remains the most popular starter on the British eating-out menu. This barbecued version is simply leagues ahead of the flaccid version in a sundae glass – but we have retained the splendid Marie Rose sauce – and don't stint on the sauce; that's the magic of a prawn cocktail.

• When you buy the prawns, make sure you ask for raw prawns, i.e. blue-grey, not pink.

• For more information on prawns, *see* page 126.

30-36 raw peeled tiger prawn, de-veined
4 x 30cm metal skewers, or equivalent

For the prawn marinade
2 tsp mild paprika
1 tbsp light olive oil or vegetable oil
1 tbsp finely chopped fresh tarragon
1/4 tsp freshly ground black pepper

After grilling
juice of 1 lemon
fine sea salt

Also for the sandwich
1 bunch watercress
1/2 cos lettuce, washed and shredded
3 spring onions, finely sliced
1 recipe quantity Marie Rose Sauce (*see* page 178)
sea salt and freshly ground black pepper
butter, softened for spreading
6 large soft granary rolls, split

To marinate the prawns Combine the marinade ingredients in a bowl. Dry the prawns thoroughly on kitchen paper and toss in the marinade, coating them well. Thread onto stainless steel skewers, skewering firstly through the thick head-end and then through the tail of each prawn. Lining up the prawns in this way makes for even cooking on the barbecue. Cover and refrigerate. Marinate for at least 2 hours; overnight is unnecessary but fine.

Before barbecuing Give the prawns enough time out of the fridge to lose their chill. Remove the thickest stems from the watercress.

Barbecue Preheat the grill to medium-high or 'sizzle' temperature. Clean and lightly oil the rack. Grill the prawn skewers for 2-3 minutes on each side until the prawns are firm, but not charred and shrinking. Be very careful, as prawns are incredibly devalued by over-cooking. They will continue to cook for a couple of minutes after you remove them from the barbecue.

To assemble the sandwich Using a fork, push the prawns off the skewers into a bowl, a couple at a time. Squeeze over some fresh lemon juice and season to taste. In a large bowl, toss the leaves and spring onions with 4 tablespoons of Marie Rose Sauce. Season the salad to taste with salt and pepper. Butter each side of the rolls. Divide the dressed leaves between the sandwich bases, top with the hot prawns, more Marie Rose Sauce (to taste) and cover with the tops. Serve immediately.

Tips If your barbecue, like the Blistering Barbecue, is designed to hold skewers above the coals without the use of racks, then do so here, as prawns are prone to stick to the grill bars.

Britain's most popular starter makes one of Blistering's most popular sandwiches.

The Blistering Build-Your-Own Beef Burger with Brie, Bacon and the Rest

MAKES 6 BURGERS

- One hour or overnight 'firming up'

- A paradox: burgers are one of the most popular snacks on the planet, but so many of them are utterly dismal. So if you make your own, pack them with all the best ingredients. Buy the best and leanest beef you can find and mince it yourself.
- Feel free to put what you like in your burger sandwich. As for sauces and relishes, just use your imagination, from tomato ketchup and mustard to Red Onion Confit (*see* page 194) and Green Tomato Chutney (*see* page 195).

For the burgers
1kg lean and preferably organic beef, minced
1 firm medium-sized onion, finely diced
3 cloves garlic, finely chopped
4 tbsp finely chopped English parsley
1 level tsp sea salt and plenty of freshly ground black pepper
vegetable oil for light brushing

For building the burger
6 slices rindless back bacon
250g ripe Brie, sliced 5mm thick
6 large floury baps, split
1 large beef tomato, sliced into rounds
80g rocket, washed and dried
sea salt and freshly ground black pepper

To assemble the burgers Place the minced beef, onion, garlic, parsley, salt and pepper in a bowl and mix well, squeezing the mince through your fingers. Divide the meat into 6 equal balls and form into burgers about 2cm thick. Using your thumb, or an egg coated in flour, make a depression in the centre of each burger about 4cm in diameter and about 1cm deep. This should ensure that the finished, grilled result is a flat, rather than a bulging burger. Cover with a layer of greaseproof paper and then clingfilm and refrigerate. Leave to firm up for an hour, or overnight.

Before barbecuing Give the burgers enough time out of the fridge to lose their chill. Brush the burgers with vegetable oil. Assemble all the other ingredients.

Barbecue Preheat the barbecue grill to medium–high or 'sizzle' temperature. Clean and lightly oil the rack. First grill the bacon: this should take no longer than $1^{1}/_{2}$ minutes on each side. Transfer to a warmed tray and cover with foil, so that it keeps warm, but doesn't dry out. For the burgers: if you are using top quality mince, it is fine to grill the burgers just to medium. To achieve this result, grill for approximately 3 minutes on each side. To cook through thoroughly, cook for a further 1-2 minutes on each side. When you have turned the burgers for the final time, place the Brie slices on the top of the burgers, where they will start to melt. No resting time is required beyond the time it takes to assemble your burgers.

To build your own burger Toast or just warm up the baps on the barbecue. Slice open the rolls fill with the Brie-covered burger. Top with salsas, relishes and sauces of your choice, bacon, slices of tomato, a scattering of rocket and any additional seasoning.

Our favourite burger combination – not too tall to get your mouth around.

The Blistering Lamb and Mint Burger with Fresh Cranberry & Orange Sauce, Mayonnaise and Watercress

MAKES 6 BURGERS

• One hour or overnight 'firming up'

• As with the beef burger, since you're going to the trouble of making them, don't stint on the quality of your meat. Lamb lends itself well to Moroccan or Indian spices, so before you go ahead and follow this recipe, check out the 'Tips' below.

• We have recommended a couple of favourite sauces here, but use your imagination to juice up your own burger as you like.

For the burgers

1kg lean and preferably organic lamb, minced
$1/2$ firm medium-sized onion, finely diced
6 spring onions, finely chopped
3 cloves garlic, finely chopped
3 tbsp finely chopped fresh mint
1 level tsp sea salt and plenty of freshly ground black pepper
vegetable oil for light brushing

To build the burger

75g watercress, tough stems removed
110g white cabbage, finely sliced
8 spring onions, finely sliced on the bias
2 tbsp Mayonnaise (*see* page 176)
$1/2$ tbsp grainy mustard
sea salt and freshly ground pepper
6 large floury baps, split
4 tbsp Fresh Cranberry & Orange Sauce (*see* page 184)
2 tbsp Mint Mojo (*see* page 190)

To assemble the burgers Place all the burger ingredients, with the exception of the vegetable oil, into a bowl and mix well, squeezing the mince through your fingers. Divide the meat into 6 equal balls and form into burgers about 2cm thick.

Using your thumb, make a depression in the centre of each burger about 4cm in diameter and about 1cm deep. This should ensure that the finished grilled result is a flat rather than a bulging burger. Cover with a layer of greaseproof paper and then clingfilm and refrigerate. Leave to firm up for an hour, or overnight.

Before barbecuing Give the burgers enough time out of the fridge to lose their chill. Brush the burgers with vegetable oil.

Assemble all the other ingredients. Place the watercress, cabbage, spring onions, mayonnaise and mustard in a bowl. Mix together into a slaw, seasoning with salt and pepper to taste.

Barbecue Preheat the barbecue grill to medium–high or 'sizzle' temperature. Clean and lightly oil the rack. If you are using top quality mince, it is fine to grill the burgers just to medium. To achieve this result, grill for 3 minutes on each side. To cook through thoroughly, cook for a further 1-2 minutes on each side. No resting time is required beyond the time it takes to assemble your burgers.

To build the burger Toast or just warm up the baps on the barbecue. Spoon Cranberry & Orange Sauce onto the base and top with the grilled lamb burger. Spoon over a little of the Mint Mojo, some of the watercress and cabbage slaw and then replace the bap top.

For a Moroccan Lamb Burger, add 2tsp ground cumin, 2tsp ground coriander, 1 tsp ground cinnamon and $1/2$ tsp cayenne pepper to the mix. Replace the mint with fresh coriander. Choose from Minted Yoghurt, Green Harissa, Pomegranate Molasses & Mint Dipping Sauce, Coriander & Ginger Pesto or Blistering Sweet Chilli Sauce to accompany it (see *Sauces and Relishes*, pp176-196).

For an Indian Lamb Burger, add 2 tsp ground cumin, 2tsp ground coriander, 1 tsp turmeric, 1 tsp toasted ground fennel, 1 tsp ground ginger, 2 tsp garam masala, 1 tsp chilli powder. Exchange the mint for fresh coriander. Choose from Salty Onion, Chilli & Lemon Relish, Shallot & Ginger Relish, or Minted Mustard Seed & Cucumber Raita, all of which are to be found in the Sauces and Relishes section of this book, or just use any of the amazing ranges of jars of pickles and chutneys available on supermarket shelves.

Grilled Haloumi, Mediterranean Vegetables and Rocket Pesto in Toasted Ciabatta

MAKES 6 LARGE SANDWICHES

- 1 or 2 night marinade

- This is a substantial and delicious summer lunch.
- Haloumi is brilliant off the barbecue: it grills and holds together perfectly. It is deliciously juicy, salty and sort-of-squeaky. But beware – it must be eaten hot straight away or it will become rubbery.

400g Haloumi cheese

For the marinade
$1/4$ red onion, finely sliced
2 cloves garlic, finely chopped
1 tbsp chopped fresh oregano
12 basil leaves, torn
$1/4$ tsp freshly ground black pepper
zest of 1 lemon
4 tbsp olive oil

Also for the sandwich
1 recipe Mediterranean Vegetable Skewers
  (*see* page 140)
3 small ciabatta loaves
Rocket Pesto (*see* page 182)

To marinate the Haloumi Combine the marinade ingredients in a bowl. Slice the Haloumi into 1cm thick wedges and place in the marinade, coating all sides. Marinate at least overnight. It will be even better after two days.

Assemble the sandwich ingredients Barbecue the Mediterranean Vegetable Skewers before you grill the cheese and ciabatta.

Either keep the vegetable skewers warm on a cooler part of the barbecue on a tray covered with foil, or push the vegetables off the skewer into a terracotta container, and cover. This way they will keep moist and continue to soften.

Barbecue A hinged sandwich rack makes grilling of small pieces of haloumi infinitely easier. Preheat the sandwich rack to medium-high or 'sizzle' temperature. Clean and lightly oil the rack. Remove the rack from the grill and fill with the Haloumi pieces. Grill the cheese for 2 minutes on the first side and for just 1 minute on the other. Don't turn the cheese until it is golden and slightly browned when it will remove more easily from the rack. If you have a removable grill rack, you may find it easier to take the rack away from the heat to turn the cheese. Work carefully and use a fish slice. When finished, transfer from the rack onto a warm plate or tray. While the cheese is grilling, lightly toast the whole ciabatta loaves on the barbecue.

To assemble the sandwich Slice open the loaves and spread each side with Rocket Pesto. Pile on the Mediterranean Vegetables, breaking up the red onion slightly if necessary and top with the freshly grilled haloumi. Slice and serve immediately while the haloumi is still warm.

You can just feel the Mediterranean lapping over your toes.

Cajun Chicken Sandwich with Avocado and Caesar Salad

MAKES 6 SANDWICHES

• 3 hour to overnight marinade

• We've tried faffing around making a good non-stick chicken burger at Blistering, which was both delicious and easy to produce in large numbers. In the end, we found that rather than messing around with bits of raw chicken, we'd rather just stick to how nature intended – a battered out chicken breast is quick, easy and succulent.
• The Cajun Spice Mix is a great one and, consisting uniquely of dried herbs and spices with a little sugar, keeps for ages in a tight-lidded jar.

6 medium-sized 110-150g skinless chicken breasts

Cajun Spice Mix (fills a 450g jam jar)
1 tbsp black peppercorns
1 tbsp white peppercorns
2 tsp dried sage
$1^1/_2$ tbsp dried oregano
$1^1/_2$ tbsp dried thyme
2 tbsp mild paprika
2 tsp cayenne pepper, or to taste
1 tbsp soft brown sugar
3 tsp garlic powder or granules

To grill
vegetable oil for brushing
fine sea salt
juice of 3 small limes

To assemble the sandwiches
juice of 1 lime
1 ripe large avocado
sea salt and freshly ground black pepper
1 small cos or romaine lettuce, washed, dried and shredded
$^1/_2$ red pepper, finely sliced
6 spring onions, finely sliced on the bias
3 tbsp Caesar Dressing (see page 176), or to taste
6 floury baps, or thickly sliced white loaf
Parmesan shavings (optional)

For the spice mix Grind the black and white peppercorns in the spice grinder until just cracked. Add the dried herbs and blitz for 5 seconds. Tip into a bowl and mix with the other ingredients. Transfer to an airtight jar.

To prepare the chicken To make the chicken sandwich-friendly, you need to flatten it out. Roll clingfilm over your chopping board. Place a chicken breast on the film and roll the film back over the top. Bash the breast out with a mallet or a rolling pin to a little over 5mm thick to make a sort of 'chicken schnitzel'. Repeat for the remaining breasts. Sprinkle each breast with one heaped teaspoon of the Cajun Spice Mix, applying it to both sides. Cover tightly with clingfilm and refrigerate for at least 3 hours, or preferably overnight.

Before barbecuing Give the chicken breasts enough time out of the fridge to lose their chill. Brush lightly with vegetable oil. Season with sea salt.

Prepare the rest of the sandwich filling Place the lime juice in a bowl. De-stone and skin the avocado and slice lengthways into the lime juice, tossing for good coverage. Season with salt and pepper. In a separate bowl, toss the lettuce, red pepper and spring onion with the Caesar Dressing.

Barbecue Preheat the barbecue grill to medium-high or 'sizzle' temperature. Clean and lightly oil the rack. Place the chicken breasts on the grill and grill for approximately 3 minutes on each side or until cooked through to the centre. Transfer the chicken to a warmed tray and squeeze the lime juice over it.

To assemble the sandwich Toast or just warm up the baps or bread slices on the barbecue. Cut the chicken down to size if necessary. Split the baps. Pile on the Caesar salad, fill with the hot chicken and top with some limey avocado, adding Parmesan shavings if desired.

Corn on the Cob with Chilli Butter

SERVES 6

- The natural sugars of corn caramelise deliciously. We've gone for Chilli Butter, but use whatever suits your mood. Do try it with our Thai Lime Chilli & Coriander Syrup (*see* page 186) for a truly great accompaniment to an oriental-themed barbecue.
- You must buy corn with the outer leaves intact and still covering the kernels. It is the biggest mistake to barbecue the raw kernels directly from the start: They will dry up and char. Leaving the leaves on allows the corn to steam in its own sweet juice.

6 corn on the cob, intact with outer leaves

Chilli Butter
110g salted butter
3 large mild red chillies, deseeded and finely chopped
$1/4$ tsp freshly ground black pepper
4 tbsp finely chopped coriander

For the Chilli Butter Place the butter, chillies and pepper in a small saucepan and leave to melt on the edge of the barbecue.

Do not allow to boil or brown.

To prepare the corn Pull off some of the outer leaves, leaving just one or two layers over the corn kernels.

Barbecue Preheat the barbecue grill to medium. Clean and lightly oil the rack. Place the corn on the grill and grill all over for approximately 30 minutes with leaves on. By the end of this time, the leaves will have charred and the kernels will have softened. Peel them right back to form a sort of dramatic husky handle. Now that the corn is exposed, baste with the Chilli Butter and carry on grilling for about 10 minutes until lightly charred all over.

To serve the corn Remove the corn to a large warmed serving bowl, brush with more of the chilli butter and scatter with the chopped coriander.

When English corn is in season and fresh, you should barbecue it like there's no tomorrow.

A Blistering Wood-fired Pizza Party

This is the perfect on-going *al fresco* party, providing entertainment and a chance to exploit your own and your guests' creative urges. It's easy on the pocket and, most importantly of all, your efforts will conjure up the most delicious results. You'll never want to order a takeaway pizza again.

Once you have mastered the art of cooking pizzas in your wood-fired oven, we guarantee that you will want to light up the oven, even in the middle of January to get your fix of the ultimate pizza. And these are fantastic pizzas: thin crusted with a great wood-fired flavour. As far as toppings go, we give you some recommendations, but a Blistering Wood-fired Pizza is whatever you make it.

'A little goes a long way'... never a truer word. With a few simple ingredients and very little outlay, you can throw a brilliant and memorable party. Once the oven is up and roaring, you will be knocking pizzas out every few minutes – or at least as quickly as you or your guests can roll out their dough and arrange their favourite toppings.

How to throw the party
Get a group of friends together – the best groups have a few children thrown in. Put drinks in their hands and provide them with some basic guidelines on how to put a pizza together. Your pizza preparation table, equipped with a bowl of floured dough, a wooden board and rolling pin along with multiple bowls of toppings will soon become the frenzied centre of attention. Find the bossiest person and make him/her the dough-rolling and pizza-making supervisor. You are manning your oven – and we promise you won't get lonely. The site of a wood-fired oven in action is mesmerising. Once you've done a test pizza, fire the starting gun – and they're off. Your guests will present you with a succession of creative and deliciously topped raw pizzas. You and your pizza shovel will be kept very busy. This kind of entertainment can go on for hours.

Blistering Pizza Party Tips

'Less is More' Keep it simple. Your guests may be inclined to lavish too much and too many varieties of topping onto their pizza bases. If a base tomato sauce is being used, a few teaspoons spread with the back of a spoon provides plenty of flavour and won't make for a soggy end result. We would recommend that you restrict the total number of topping varieties to five or six at the very very most, including the tomato sauce. One of the favourite Blistering combinations is sliced tomato, sliced garlic and basil – so simple, but perfectly delicious!

'You can never be too thin' To achieve a thin crispy base, and to cook through within the few minutes allocated to each masterpiece, the dough must be rolled out very thinly.

Look after the edges For a delicious crunchy crust, leave about 1.5cm of dough edge topping-free to drizzle with extra virgin olive oil and sprinkle with sea salt. Make sure you rotate the pizza during cooking to prevent scorching the edge.

Wood-fired pizzas are so crisp and delicious. You'll never want to order a take-away pizza again. This is the perfect *al fresco* party.

Top ingredients

Resist the urge to buy a packet mix for the base and make your own pizza dough. The effort pays off. Invest in some good quality toppings – a tasty extra virgin olive oil makes a big difference. Don't buy rubbery blocks of mozzarella; find some of the juicy, stringy buffalo variety. And tomatoes? Forget the intensively grown standard supermarket variety and go for the richer plum, bulbous beef or explosive cherry tomatoes.

'Mise en Place'

A Blistering Pizza Party looks easy and it is, but only if you organise yourself beforehand. Allow at leat an hour for this. It's all about *mise en place* – the chef's term for having your equipment and ingredients lined up and ready for action!

Blistering Pizza Party Equipment

The Pizza preparation table

- The pizza dough
- 2 wooden chopping boards – one for rolling the dough, the other for cutting the finished pizza
- rolling pin
- bowl of flour
- bowl of salt
- pepper grinder
- small bowls and plates of toppings
- bottle of extra virgin olive oil – with pourer if you have one
- pizza cutting wheel
- pile of small plates
- pile of paper napkins

The Wood-fired oven

- Logs, charcoal and all the usual (*see* page 12)
- Pizza shovel
- Oven-proof cloth
- Poker or small metal rake to pull forward the embers
- Horse hair or natural fibre brush to brush back the embers

Blistering Pizza Toppings

Here are some
recommendations, but don't
let us cramp your style.

- Parma or Serrano ham
- Sliced smoked ham
- Sliced smoked chicken
- Sliced chorizo or pepperoni
- Wood-smoked fresh salmon
- Prawns
- Salted anchovies
- Fresh thinly sliced tuna
- Buffalo Mozzarella
- Gorgonzola

- Mascarpone
- Parmesan shavings
- Cottage cheese or ricotta
- Crème fraiche
- Capers
- Red peppers, finely sliced
- Red onions, finely sliced
- Fresh pineapple
- Spring onions, sliced
- Raw garlic, finely sliced
- Wild or field mushrooms, sliced
- Baby artichoke hearts in oil
- Wood-roast Mediterranean
  Vegetables (*see* page 152)

- Wood-roast sweet potato
- Sweet corn
- Sliced fresh tomatoes
- Fresh rocket
- Fresh baby spinach
- Basil
- Oregano
- Thyme leaves
- Salmariglio (*see* page 182)
- Rocket Pesto (*see* page 182)
- Homemade Tomato Sauce
  (*see* opposite)
- Flavoured extra virgin olive oil

Some Favourite Blistering Wood-fired Pizzas

'Italiano' Tomato sauce, Parma
ham, Buffalo Mozzarella, fresh
rocket, garlic, oil, sea salt and
freshly ground black pepper.

Simple Tomato Fresh tomato
(thinly sliced), fresh garlic (thinly
sliced), basil leaves, olive oil,
sea salt and freshly ground black
pepper.

'Tarte Flambée' Mascarpone,
cottage cheese, red onions (finely
sliced), garlic (finely sliced), thyme,
wood-roast artichokes.

Homemade Tomato Sauce for Pizza

ENOUGH FOR 12 SMALL PIZZAS

• This freezes well, so make up a big batch and use it for pastas too.

1 scant tbsp olive oil
1 medium onion, finely chopped
3 cloves garlic, finely chopped
2 tsp tomato purée
400g can chopped plum tomatoes
1/2 tsp sugar
2 tsp fresh thyme leaves
sea salt and freshly ground pepper to taste

Heat the oil in a stainless steel or non-stick pan. Cook the onions and garlic in the oil on a medium heat, stirring occasionally, for 5 minutes or so or until soft and golden, but not browned. Stir in the tomato purée and cook, stirring for a minute. Add the chopped tomatoes, sugar and thyme, turn down the heat and simmer gently for 20 minutes to 'cook out' the tomatoes. Add a little water if the sauce is becoming too thick. Blend if you want a smooth sauce. Season to taste.

Pizza Dough

ENOUGH FOR 24 SMALL, THIN, CRISPY PIZZAS (TO SERVE 6)

800g strong white bread flour
1 tsp salt
30g dried active baking yeast
2 tsp of sugar
425ml warm water
approximately 1 tbsp olive oil

Put the flour and salt in a large bowl. Mix the yeast with the sugar and the 100 ml of warm water in a bowl or jug. Cover with clingfilm and stand the mixture in a warm, draught-free place. After 10-15 minutes the mixture will have frothed up. Whisk and add to the flour and salt with the rest of the water. Stir in the liquid and mix to a dough. Though the dough will stick to your hands initially, you will soon find that it just peels off.

Knead the dough for 10-15 minutes or until it is smooth and elastic. Use an electric cake mixer with the dough hook if you have one. If you cut through the dough with a knife,

the air bubbles should be of fairly even size. If the dough becomes sticky, add a little more flour. Form the dough into a ball and brush with olive oil. Cover with a damp cloth and leave it in a warm place for 1-2 hours, or until doubled in size. During this rising process, you should be preparing your toppings. Light your wood-fired oven 45 minutes to an hour before you're going to start cooking your pizzas to get it good and hot.

Punch back the dough and knead it for a minute to get rid of some of the excess air. Cover with clingfilm and leave to one side. You don't want it to rise again before use. If it does so in the heat of the day, just knock it back again.

To make an individual thin pizza, roll out a ball of dough weighing 40-50g into a rough circle to a thickness of around just 2mm. Use a well floured board and, of course, make sure that your pizza is no bigger than the pizza shovel.

Blistering Wood-fired Pizza – the method

Preparing the oven Experience is the key here. The first time you use your oven, don't expect total success immediately. You should know your stuff by the time you're onto your third pizza. You'll be surprised at how soon you will become an expert with your own oven.

You need a fire with 3 or 4 small logs to start you off. After about 30-40 minutes, your logs will have burnt down and blackened and will be generating a large amount of heat. This is the heat you're after. From this point onwards, you will need to add a small log every 15-20 minutes or so, to maintain the heat. You may use charcoal if you prefer. These timings are approximate and will vary according to how well-seasoned your logs are and obviously on their size. Also note that a windy day may speed things up considerably.

You will be maintaining the fire at the back of the oven and cooking the pizza on the base at the front. Before placing the pizza in the oven, you need to make the oven base as hot as possible. To this end, rake or pull the wood embers from the back of the oven forward over the base where you will cook the pizza. Leave the embers to burn for 3-4 minutes and brush them back again to give a relatively clean terracotta base.

To top the pizza If using tomato sauce (*see* recipe on page 71), use no more than 3 tsp spread over the dough with the back of the spoon, leaving a crust of about 1.5cm. Remembering the tenet that 'less is more', scatter over a few toppings, drizzle the edges in particular with a little extra virgin olive oil and season to taste with sea salt and freshly ground pepper. Inch and shuffle your well-floured pizza shovel under the pizza ready to transfer it to the hot floor of your wood fired oven.

To wood-roast the pizza Slide and shuffle the pizza off the floured shovel onto the base and watch it cook (incredibly quickly!). Give it approximately 1 minute, or until the rear crust, which is nearer to the fire, begins to colour. At this point, slide the shovel under the pizza and quickly rotate the pizza through 180 degrees. Slide back onto the oven base. Leave for a further minute or so, or until cooked and then retrieve it from the oven. Slide the cooked pizza onto the cutting board and leave it to be sliced with the pizza-cutting wheel. Carry on to the next pizza like a pro.

BIRDS

Blistering Barbecued Chicken Thighs with Blistering Sweet and Sticky Barbecue Sauce

SERVES 6

- 3 hour to overnight marinade

- The secret to this dish is in the two-layer marinade. The second marinade is simply Blistering Sweet and Sticky Barbecue Sauce.
- Boneless chicken thighs are a Blistering favourite. Don't feel restricted to this terrific marinade – you could use any marinade from any recipe in this book.
- Thighs have a higher fat content than the breast and will stay moist grilled on the barbecue. We always cook thighs boneless, as they cook more quickly and you don't have the worry of them not grilling all the way through to the bone. Since our butcher at Blistering doesn't seem to mind boning tens of thousands of chicken thighs over the summer season, we feel sure that your butcher should willingly bone a dozen for you.

12 chicken thighs, skin-on, boneless

Marinade One
1½ tbsp mild sweet paprika
1½ tbsp soft dark brown sugar
3 tsp garlic powder
3 tbsp Worcestershire Sauce
2 tsp dried oregano

Marinade Two
6 tbsp Blistering Sweet and Sticky Barbecue Sauce (*see* page 184)

sea salt and freshly ground pepper

To marinate the thighs Mix Marinade One ingredients to a paste in a bowl and spread it over the thighs. Using disposable gloves, massage the paste into the meat. Spoon over Marinade Two, again rubbing in thoroughly. Cover and refrigerate overnight or for at least 3 hours.

Before barbecuing Give the thighs enough time out of the fridge to lose their chill. Season with salt and pepper as desired.

Barbecue Preheat the barbecue sandwich rack to medium-high. Clean and lightly oil the rack. Place the chicken thighs, smooth skin-side up, with the loose skin tucked underneath onto the hot grill. Grill for two minutes on each side before moving to a medium heat. Continue to grill for approximately 4–5 minutes on each side, or until cooked through. Chicken thighs vary in size, so cooking time can vary.

To serve Place on a serving dish. Serve traditionally with your choice of slaw, potato salad and Blistering Sweet and Sticky Barbecue Sauce.

Tips To add a more interesting smoky flavour, try throwing hickory chips into the barbecue halfway through cooking. (Soak the chips in water for a couple of hours before using.) Then, to serve, place on a dish and douse with lemon juice and a sprinkling of fresh tarragon. Accompany with Roasted Tomato Salsa (*see* page 192).

The ultimate barbecue marinade and sauce with the ultimate barbecue meat – the most popular barbecue dish on the planet!

Chicken Thighs with Lemon, Tarragon and Garlic served with Roasted Tomato, Oregano & Red Onion Salsa

SERVES 6

• 3 hour to overnight marinade

• Unless it is very last minute, never put lemon juice into any meat or fish marinade, as it breaks down the meat fibres 'cooking' the meat.

12 chicken thighs, skin-on, boneless

For the marinade
3 tbsp chopped tarragon
finely grated zest of 2-3 lemons
8-10 cloves garlic, finely chopped
2 tbsp olive oil
3 tbsp water

sea salt and freshly ground pepper
juice of 2 lemons
sprinkling of fresh tarragon, finely chopped
Roasted Tomato, Oregano & Red Onion Salsa
  (see page 192)

Mix the marinade ingredients in a bowl or a blender.

Open out the chicken thighs, exposing the inner flesh. Thoroughly coat the chicken with the marinade, inside and out. Re-roll the thighs and arrange on a plate. Cover and refrigerate for at least 3 hours, or preferably overnight.

Season the chicken on both sides with salt and pepper just before grilling.

Barbecue *See* barbecue instructions for Blistering Barbecued Chicken Thighs (*see* page 74).

To serve Place on a serving dish. Douse with the lemon juice and sprinkle over a little fresh tarragon. Serve with Roasted Tomato, Oregano & Red Onion Salsa (*see* page 74).

Tips The marinade will keep in the fridge for a few days. Try serving with Green Tomato Chutney (*see* page 195) or Roughly Chopped Fresh Green Salsa (*see* page 192). As an alternative, instead of lemons and tarragon use limes, fresh coriander and dried chilli flakes.

A magical, quick and classical marinade, which is so much more than just the sum of its parts.

Spatchcocked Thai Poussin with Coriander and Ginger served with Chilled Coconut, Lime & Coriander Sauce

SERVES 6

- 3 hour to overnight marinade

- A spatchcocked poussin is opened out and flattened making for quicker and more even barbecuing. As well as looking dramatic, being cooked on the bone is a particularly succulent way to eat chicken. This recipe is also great with simple chicken thighs.

6 poussins, spatchcocked
30 x 15cm bamboo skewers, or equivalent

For the marinade
3 stems lemon grass
6 lime leaves
225g sugar
150ml water
4 cloves garlic, finely chopped
2 thumbs ginger, finely chopped
1 tbsp dried shrimp, ground (optional)
6 stars of star anise
2 birdseye chillies with seeds left in, finely sliced
4 tbsp fish sauce (nam pla)
generous bunch fresh coriander, roughly chopped leaves and several stems.

sea salt and freshly ground pepper
juice of 2 limes

Peel off the outer yellow leaves of the lemon grass and trim the top. Cut each stem on the diagonal into 5 or 6 pieces. Shred or tear the lime leaves. Neither lemon grass nor lime leaves are meant to be eaten, so the pieces should be of a size that can be picked out by your guests.

Make a syrup by stirring the sugar and water in a pan over a gentle heat. Once the sugar has dissolved, and not before, bring the syrup to the boil and allow to simmer gently for 3 minutes before turning off the heat. Add all the marinade ingredients, with the exception of the fresh coriander and leave to cool. Once cool, or nearly cool, stir in the coriander.

To spatchcock a poussin Place a poussin on a chopping board, breast side down. Using poultry shears or good kitchen scissors, cut along each side of the backbone and remove it. This will partially open up the bird. You need to break the wishbone, so either snip it with the scissors, or place the poussin flat on the board and push down on the wishbone to snap it. Cut 1cm or so into the breastbone to allow the bird to flatten out completely. Now tidy up the bird by snipping off its wing tips and leg knuckles.

If, as we do at Blistering, you would prefer to use a heavy sharp knife, hold the bird firmly on a chopping board breast-side up. Insert the knife into the cavity of the Poussin and cut down hard either side of the unwanted backbone and discard it. Insert the knife a little further and break the wishbone. Cut through some of the breastbone if necessary to flatten the bird out totally.

To hold the birds in the spatchcocked shape Feed bamboo skewers in a cross shape through the birds. Coat the birds with the cooled marinade. Cover and refrigerate overnight or for at least 3 hours.

Give the poussins enough time out of the fridge to lose their chill. Season with salt and pepper as required. Reserve the excess marinade.

A truly authentic Bangkok street food experience.

Barbecue Preheat the barbecue grill or sandwich rack to medium. Clean and lightly oil the rack. Place the spatchcocked poussins bone-side down first. Grill for a total of 12-15 minutes, turning every 3-4 minutes. Poussins vary in size, so cooking time can vary. Test for 'doneness' by inserting the point of a small sharp knife. Remove from the grill onto a warmed tray. Squeeze lime juice over them and leave to rest for a few minutes.

Reduce down the marinade to make a sauce Place the excess marinade in a pan and bring to the boil. Add 8-10 tbsp of water and simmer for 7 minutes to be sure that any contamination from the raw chicken has been killed off.

To serve Place the cooked poussins on a serving dish and pour over the cooked marinade mixture. Delicious served with a light fresh Thai Salad with Green Papaya (*see* page 166).

Tips For extra stickiness, you may choose to drizzle some of the marinade over the poussins halfway through the barbecuing process. If you can get hold of them, this dish looks great served on banana leaves. If available, quail makes for a great alternative.

Whole Boned Portuguese Spicy Piri Piri Chicken with Lemons and Herbs and Sour Cream & Chives

SERVES 6

• 3 hour to overnight marinade

- One of Portugal's national dishes and not for the faint hearted, this is a stunning hot and spicy centrepiece to any barbecue party.
- Your butcher will bone a chicken for you. A boned chicken allows you to open out the bird to brush marinade into every nook and cranny. Roll the meat back up, tied or not, to give you a succulent barbecued dish that is hassle-free to carve.
- Chicken must be cooked all the way through before serving, and this is a substantial chicken joint, so it is important to have a barbecue with the facility to control temperature using grill height or a lid. We would also recommend the use of a temperature probe.

1 boned out 1.8-2.5kg chicken

For the marinade
1$\frac{1}{2}$ tbsp vegetable oil
6 cloves garlic, finely chopped
6 large red chillies, including seeds, finely chopped
3 tbsp light brown sugar
1$\frac{1}{2}$ tbsp white wine vinegar
4 tbsp tomato ketchup
2 tbsp tomato purée
3 tbsp Worcestershire Sauce
6 tbsp water
3 tbsp fresh oregano, chopped

sea salt and freshly ground pepper
3 lemons, cut into wedges
sprinkling of fresh chilli, finely chopped (optional)
Sour Cream & Chives (*see* page 190)

For the marinade Heat the oil in a small heavy-bottomed pan. Fry the garlic and chillies on a medium heat for 1 minute. Add all the other ingredients with the exception of the oregano, and bring to the boil. Turn off and leave to cool. Once cool, or almost cool, add the oregano.

Open out the whole boned-out chicken, exposing the inner flesh. Thoroughly coat the chicken with two thirds of the cooled marinade, inside and out. (You are holding back one third of the marinade for basting). Fold the chicken into its original shape. Cover and refrigerate for at least 3 hours, or preferably overnight.

Season the chicken with salt and pepper just before grilling. We would strongly recommend that you use a hinged barbecue sandwich rack to hold the chicken in shape during grilling. If you grill the bird directly on the barbecue rack, it may unfold.

Barbecue Preheat the barbecue to medium. Clean and lightly oil the rack. Place the chicken, smooth skin-side up, with the loose skin tucked underneath onto the hot grill, preferably held in shape in a hinged barbecue sandwich rack. Grill on this side for 5-7 minutes or until the skin is sealed and starting to colour. Turn the chicken over and grill for a further 5-7 minutes. Continue to grill on both sides, turning every 5-7 minutes until

A personality-packed dish – not for the faint-hearted.

the chicken is cooked, basting with the reserved marinade. Total grill times will vary, but should lie somewhere between 30 and 40 minutes. When cooked, a temperature probe will reach 72C in the centre of the bird.

To serve Rest the bird for 10 minutes, covered with tin foil. Carve on a large wooden board in front of your guests.

Place on a serving dish surrounded with lemon wedges and scatter with even more chilli if desired. Serve with Sour Cream & Chives.

Tips Great served with Avocado and Baby Leaf Salad dressed with Lime and Coriander. Try serving with thin-cut skin-on fresh potato chips fried in olive oil... delicious.

Chicken Breast stuffed with Porcini Mushrooms, Pancetta, Mozzarella and Sage served with Roasted Garlic Mayonnaise
SERVES 6

• Firm up the chicken breasts in the fridge for at least 2 hours

• Chicken breasts can tend to dry out on the barbecue, but with a little help from a stuffing, and a resistance to overcooking, you can achieve a tender and juicy result. At Blistering, we prefer 'French-trimmed' breasts with their protruding trimmed wing bone. They just look great on the plate. We think that if you're going to go to the effort of stuffing a breast, it's worth a few minutes more work (for your butcher, not for you).

6 chicken breasts, preferably organic and/or cornfed, 'French-trimmed'

For the stuffing
1 tbsp olive oil
3 cloves garlic, finely chopped
160g pancetta, cut into 5mm dice
160g fresh porcini mushrooms (ceps), thinly sliced
12 sage leaves, finely chopped
1 ball Buffalo Mozzarella, finely chopped
sea salt and freshly ground pepper

sea salt and freshly ground pepper
a little olive oil

For the stuffing Heat the oil in a frying pan. Fry the garlic on a medium heat for a minute or so, stirring. Add the pancetta and continue to cook for another couple of minutes until sealed and beginning to colour, but not crispy. Add the mushrooms and sage and continue to cook for three minutes on a medium to low heat. Turn off and leave to cool. Once cool, stir in the Mozzarella. Season to taste. Cover and refrigerate. The stuffing must be thoroughly chilled before stuffing the breasts.

Place the chicken breasts flesh–side down on a chopping board. Peel back the skin. You'll find that one side of the skin flap peels back readily, with the other side being held more firmly to the flesh with connective tissue. Place a spoonful of the stuffing under and skin and stretch the skin back over the stuffing. Repeat with the other five breasts, using up all the stuffing. Cover and refrigerate for at least 2 hours to firm up.

Remove from the fridge around 20 minutes before grilling. Season the chicken with salt and pepper and lightly brush the undersides with olive oil.

Barbecue You must be careful not to overcook chicken breasts, as their low fat content means that they will rapidly become dry and unappealing. Preheat the barbecue to medium. Clean and lightly oil the rack. Place the chicken breasts on the barbecue grill or sandwich rack, stuffed skin-side up. Grill the flesh side for 5-7 minutes before turning. Grill on the skin side for a further 4-6 minutes, or until the breasts are cooked

through. Cooking times will vary with the size of the breasts. Test with the point of a small sharp knife to check the breast is cooked through.

To serve Rest the breasts for 3-4 minutes, covered with tin foil. Serve with Roasted Garlic Mayonnaise (*see* page 178).

Tips If fresh porcini mushrooms aren't available, you could use a combination of soaked dried porcini mushrooms mixed with fresh field mushrooms, or, if you can get hold of them, frozen porcini mushrooms make an excellent standby.

Asian Duck with Sweet Soy, Star Anise, Ginger, Coriander and Palm Sugar served with Asian Top Shelf Sauce   SERVES 6

• 3 hour to overnight marinade

• Duck breasts are simply fantastic grilled on the barbecue. Ask your butcher for female rather than male duck breasts, as they make for the perfect portion size. The skin is very fatty (how else would ducks keep warm in winter waters?), so will need some keen trimming.
• Asian Top Shelf Sauce (*see* p188) lasts for weeks, so make up a jar and keep it on your larder shelf.

6 duck breasts, preferably female

For the marinade
75g palm sugar or light brown sugar
3 tbsp water
6 stars of star anise
2 thumbs fresh ginger, peeled and finely chopped
6 tbsp sweet soy sauce (or Ketjap Manis)
1 tbsp chopped coriander stem
1 tbsp sesame oil
$1/2$ tsp dried chilli flakes, or to taste

3 tbsp chopped coriander leaves

To prepare the duck There is a lot of fat on duck breasts, which if not trimmed down will result in dramatic flaming and consequent unwanted smoking. Place the duck breasts skin side down on the chopping board. Run your fingers along between the fatty skin and the meat to begin to separate the two. Keeping the breasts skin side down, trim the loose fat off to around 5mm from the edges of the meat on each side and at the top and the bottom of each breast. Do not trim off any of the meat. Turn the breast skin side up and score the fat at 1cm intervals, criss-crossed on a diagonal, giving a diamond harlequin pattern.

For the marinade Melt the palm sugar in a pan with the water and star anise. When the sugar has melted, take the pan off the heat and add the other marinade ingredients. Allow the marinade to cool completely before thoroughly coating the duck breasts on both sides. Cover and refrigerate for at least

Duck is a robust meat with lots of flavour, crying out for sweet, sticky marinades.

3 hours, or preferably overnight. Remove from the fridge around 20 minutes before grilling.

Barbecue Duck is at its most tender when cooked pink, so be careful not to overcook it. Preheat the barbecue to medium. Clean and lightly oil the rack. For a pink-medium result, place the duck breasts skin-side down on the brushed and oiled barbecue grill or sandwich rack. Grill for 4-5 minutes to produce a crispy skin before turning. Grill on the flesh side for a further 4-5 minutes. Place on a warm plate or tray, cover with foil (leaving a gap to allow steam to escape) and let the duck rest for at least 5 minutes before carving.

To serve Carve each breast on an angle into 2-3 pieces and scatter with fresh, chopped coriander leaves. Serve with rice or noodles, Chargrilled Bok Choi and Red Peppers marinated in Thai Lime, Chilli & Coriander Syrup (*see* page 149) and Asian Top Shelf Sauce on the side.

Tips As an alternative, try serving the duck with Mango Lime & Mint Salsa (*see* page 191). The sharp fruity flavour cuts the sweet stickiness of the duck beautifully.

Middle Eastern Spiced Quail, served with Green Harissa and Minted Yoghurt

SERVES 6

• 3 hour to overnight marinade

• Spectacular when piled high on a Blistering Buffet or exciting as a plated supper, quail is sweet, tender, and slightly gamey. You can either spatchcock the quail (see Poussin recipe, page 76) or if you have good temperature control on your barbecue, just leave them as they are.

• Preserved lemons impart a unique flavour to this marinade and are available in specialist stores (see Suppliers appendix, page 215).

12 quail, as they are or spatchcocked

For the marinade
1 tbsp coriander seeds
2 tbsp cumin seeds
3 cloves
8-10 cm cinnamon stick, broken up
12 peppercorns
3 tsp sumac
$\frac{1}{2}$ tsp grated nutmeg
2 tbsp mild paprika
zest of 2 lemons or 1 finely chopped preserved lemon
3 tbsp pomegranate molasses
1 onion, blended in a food processor or grated
4 garlic cloves, finely chopped
3 tbsp vegetable oil
3 tbsp chopped fresh parsley
3 tbsp chopped fresh coriander

sea salt and freshly ground pepper
4 tbsp pistachio nuts, chopped
Green Harissa (see page 196)
Middle Eastern Minted Yoghurt (see page 196)

For the marinade Toast the coriander and cumin seeds, cloves, cinnamon and peppercorns in a heated dry frying pan or skillet, or in a medium oven until aromatic. Blitz to a coarse powder in your spice grinder. Mix with the remaining marinade ingredients. Coat the quails with the thick marinade and rub into the birds' cavities. Cover and refrigerate for at least three hours, or preferably overnight.

Allow the quail at least 20 minutes out of the refrigerator to lose their chill before barbecuing. Season with salt and pepper just before grilling.

Barbecue Preheat the barbecue to medium. Clean and lightly oil the rack.

For whole quail Place the birds on the brushed and oiled barbecue grill. Grill on each of its four sides for about 3 minutes to begin the cooking process and to pick up some colour. Line the quail up on the grill, breast side up and cover with a lid, or foil, and continue to cook on a medium grill for around 6 minutes, or until the birds are cooked through. Test them by pulling at one of the legs. If it comes away freely, the birds are ready.

For spatchcocked quail Grill on each side for 4-5 minutes on a medium heat, turning to prevent scorching.

To serve Rest the birds for 5 minutes, covered with tin foil. Pile on a serving dish and scatter with chopped pistachio nuts. Serve with Middle Eastern Minted Yoghurt and Green Harissa, accompanied with Cous Cous Salad (see page 161),

Tips You'll need piles of paper napkins and lime finger bowls to keep your guests happy.

Quail is great for taste and value, and very quick to grill on the barbecue.

Provencale Guinea Fowl Breast wrapped in Poitrine Fumée with Rosemary, Lemon and Garlic served with Fresh Tomato Salsa

SERVES 6

• 3 hour to overnight marinade

• Guinea fowl is an under-exploited commodity. In the barbecued breast league, guinea fowl beats chicken 2-1. It has more flavour (1-0), a higher fat content (2-0), but is slightly more expensive (2-1). Here we suggest French trimming for guinea fowl breast as in the Chicken Breast with Porcini Mushrooms recipe (see page 79). Note that guinea fowl bones tend to be more brittle than chicken bones, so the knuckle bone must be left intact.

• *Poitrine Fumée* is as close to bacon as the French get. If you can't get hold of any, use top quality (i.e. not pumped full of water) rindless streaky bacon as a good second best.

6 guinea fowl breasts, French trimmed
12 cocktail sticks

For the marinade
6 cloves garlic, finely chopped
zest of 2 lemons
3 tbsp rosemary oil (infuse gently warmed olive oil with rosemary sprigs, garlic and peppercorns. Also available from all delis and good supermarkets)

6 slices *poitrine fumée* bacon
6 x 15cm stems rosemary
sea salt and freshly ground pepper
juice of 2 lemons

Mix the marinade ingredients.

Place the guinea fowl on a chopping board and trim off any excess skin or fat. Put to one side. Before wrapping the *poitrine fumée* bacon around the breast, you need to stretch it. Lay the strips of *poitrine* on the board.

Hold on to one end of the strip and using the blunt back side of a knife run the knife firmly along its length to stretch it out long and thin. Repeat with all six strips.

Lay a rosemary stem on each of the guinea fowl breasts and wrap the poitrine around the breast in a spiral fashion, securing it into place either end with cocktail sticks. Repeat with all six breasts. Brush over the marinade, cover and refrigerate for at least 3 hours or overnight.

Before barbecuing Give the marinaded breasts enough time out of the fridge to lose their chill. Season with salt and pepper as required.

Barbecue Preheat the barbecue grill or sandwich rack to medium. Clean and lightly oil the rack. Place the breasts on the barbecue and cook each side for 4–5 minutes or until cooked through. Stir 6 tablespoons of water into the dregs of the marinade and baste the breasts after 2–3 minutes. Allow the breasts to rest for 5 minutes before serving.

To serve Remove the cocktail sticks from the cooked breasts and place on a serving dish. Pour the lemon juice over them. For a terrific summer lunch, serve with Yellow and Green Courgette Salad (see page 174), Fresh Tomato Salsa (see page 193) and focaccia bread toasted on the barbecue.

Tips You can use any garden herbs on this one – thyme, oregano, bay leaves all make for delicious flavours.

Wood-roast Christmas Goose stuffed with Sausage Meat, Apricot and Chestnuts served with Wood-roast Potatoes and Vegetables SERVES 6

- Once the presents have been opened, many of us are looking for a way to get out of the house on Christmas Day. We recommend the peace and quiet of the back garden, a glass of wine, a wood-fired oven and the aroma of a roasting goose. You may find that you won't be alone for long! One of the advantages of a wood-fired oven over a barbecue is that if it rains (or snows!) the fire won't go out. Pop up a garden umbrella, grab a coat and get on with it.
- Goose breast is a delicate meat, contrasting sharply with the robust and flavourful leg. It makes sense to cook the two parts separately.

1 x approximately 5kg fresh goose

For the stuffing
1 tbsp vegetable oil
1 medium Spanish onion, finely diced
2 cloves garlic, finely chopped
3 tsp chopped fresh thyme
2 tbsp brandy
175g dried apricots, roughly chopped
75g cooked, peeled chestnuts, roughly chopped
  (a great canned product readily available)
zest of 1 orange
500g good quality sausage meat
$1/2$ tsp sea salt and plenty of freshly ground pepper

sea salt and freshly ground pepper
2 tsp fresh thyme leaves
1 large glass white wine

For the stuffing Heat the oil in a frying pan or heavy-bottomed stainless steel pan. Cook the onions, garlic and thyme, without colour, on a medium heat for 2-3 minutes, stirring occasionally.

Add the brandy and flame with a match. Take off the heat and stir in the apricots, chestnuts and orange zest. Cool the mixture before mixing with the sausage meat, and salt and pepper. Disposable gloves come in very handy here for thorough blending of the stuffing ingredients.

Preparing the bird for roasting Using a sharp knife, cut off both legs. Slash the fatty skin of the leg three times, season with salt and pepper and sprinkle with thyme leaves. Place the legs on a grill rack over an oven tray, so that during the cooking process the rendered fat can drip off the legs into the tray below. This fat can be used later for roasting the potatoes and other root vegetables. Stuff your goose carcass with the sausage meat stuffing and place on an oven tray. Splash with a large glass of white wine, which helps to both flavour the meat and to keep it moist. Season the carcass with salt and pepper

Wood-roasting the bird Light the oven according to the instructions on page 24. This is a labour of love. Roast the legs on the bottom of the oven (relatively cooler part of the oven) for $1^1/2$ to $1^3/4$ hours, turning the tray and turning over the legs for even cooking at $1/4$ hour intervals, basting with the excess fat from the drip tray. Place the stuffed bird on the shelf or 'trivet'. This is the hotter part of the oven. You will need to turn the tray front to back every 7-8 minutes for the first 20-25 minutes while the breasts gain colour. Cover the bird with foil and keep turning every $1/4$ hour, basting with excess juices for approximately $1^1/2$ hours or until cooked through.

The sausage meat stuffing must be cooked through to the middle, showing a temperature of 72C on completion. Let the goose rest in a warm oven (around 60C) while you wood-roast the vegetables and potatoes. You may need to splash a little more wine into the tray if it is drying up and burning.

To serve Carving the legs can be a bit of a messy business, so we would suggest that you do this in the kitchen and lay the darker meat around the uncarved carcass. Carve the breasts and spoon out the stuffing at the table.

Serve with Wood-roast Potatoes (*see* page 157) Autumnal Wood-roast Roots (*see* page 150) and homemade Cranberry and Orange Sauce (*see* page 184).

Tips If you want to roast potatoes and root vegetables in the goose fat in the wood-fired oven (and it would be a crime not to), then free up some space and transfer the roasting legs to your kitchen oven (preheat to 180C) halfway through cooking. They will already have picked up a fantastic wood-roast flavour.

This will definitely be one of the most delicious and memorable Christmas dinners you have ever tasted.

MEAT

Lamb:
Butterflied Leg, Chops and Steaks

Butterflied Leg of Lamb

Full of flavour and with a good fat content to keep the meat moist during the grilling process, leg of lamb is one of the best big joints of meat to cook on a barbecue. A 'butterflied' leg is boned and opened out. An average leg of lamb has a weight of around 2.3kg with the bone in and 1.7 kg when butterflied. This is plenty to feed 8 people. Make sure that you carve it to order to maintain the juiciness and heat of the remaining joint.

The butterflying process This process has many advantages. Firstly, for the marinating process, you have easy access to the interior of the meat, allowing for more thorough flavouring. Secondly, the opening out and removal of the bone allows for easier and brisker grilling control, so that armed with a temperature probe, you can easily monitor progress, cooking the meat as pink or well done as you like. Thirdly, it is abundantly easier to slice and serve on the barbecue buffet, with everybody having a luscious slice of juicy meat and a thin layer of crispy flavoured fat.

Ask your butcher to remove the bone, butterfly and trim your leg of lamb. What you'll get resembles a somewhat gory butterfly, in so much as it consists roughly of two flattened out wings of flesh (or lobes), joined by a thinner piece that originally ran along the bone.

The marinating process For the tastiest results, start the marinating process the day or even two days before, rubbing the meat on all sides with your chosen marinade. Roll it up and pack it in a plastic bag, or in a bowl covered with clingfilm. Refrigerate overnight, or for at the very least four hours. As a rule of thumb, Blistering do not add salt to marinades. Salt draws water out of the meat, making for a less succulent finished result. You will find that some marinades contain salty ingredients such as soy sauce, but experience has shown that they have no noticeable ill effects.

To barbecue a butterflied leg of lamb
Remove the lamb from the fridge, unfold the butterflied meat and re-cover with clingfilm half an hour or so before barbecuing to lose the chill of the fridge. Season all over on both sides with salt and pepper as required.

The barbecuing process can be summarised into stages of sealing, cooking and basting and then – just as important as the cooking process – resting.

Barbecue Heat the barbecue grill to medium-high, or 'sizzle' temperature. Using a wire brush, brush the grill to remove any stubborn charred-on bits from previous sessions. Most will have burnt off at this point. Taking great care to keep your fingers clear of the hot bars, rub the grill with a lightly oiled cloth. Place the meat on the barbecue grill and seal the meat on both sides until lightly browned. This should take about 4-5 minutes on each side. As a general rule, do not use a fork to turn the meat, as puncturing the surface of the joint at this point will result in losing juices. Always use tongs, as you will be turning the meat many times. Once the meat is sealed, slow the grilling process down to medium or 'cook' temperature. Do this either by moving the meat to a cooler area, by using a lid, or if you have the facility, by adjusting the height of the meat above the coals. Continue to cook on a medium heat, turning the lamb every 5-7 minutes or so to prevent scorching.

A butterflied leg of lamb is, without doubt, one of the best big joints to grill on the barbecue.

Garlic Brine Baste

- At Blistering, we have picked up an idea commonly used in Argentina and other South American countries where the meat is basted with a light garlic brine. This adds garlic flavour and seasoning. It also cools down the fat, which would otherwise run off the lamb and ignite on the coals. Most importantly, it helps to produce a beautifully juicy result.

20g sea salt
500ml water
6 cloves garlic, finely chopped

Mix the salt with the water. Add the garlic. Baste the meat every 7-8 minutes.

Grill times for butterflied leg of lamb
30-40 minutes should give you a beautifully rosy medium-cooked result. A temperature probe inserted into the middle of the thickest part of the meat should read 50-55C. Rest for at least 20 minutes, covered with a double layer of tin foil, leaving a small air hole for steam to escape, for the lamb to turn a rosy colour. The air hole is there to prevent the steam from cooking the lamb any further. During the resting process, the sinews relax and absorb the juices. To cut into the meat without resting it would allow the juices to stream out of the meat leaving it dry and unappealing.

Four Lamb Marinades for Butterflied Legs, Chops and Steaks

ENOUGH FOR 16 LAMB CHOPS

Here are some of our favourite lamb overnight marinades – but do experiment and try them on other meats, fish and vegetables. If you would like to make one of the spice flavours more pronounced, don't be afraid to play around with the recipe quantities.

This is how new and fantastic recipes are created.

All marinade quantities are sufficient for a 1.7kg (boned weight) butterflied leg of lamb, 16 lamb chops (approximately 2kg) or 1.7 kg of lamb steaks.

1) Indian Masala

- We love Indian spices, and lamb carries them brilliantly. In India, meat is traditionally cooked over naked flame, or wood-fired in a Tandoori oven. Serve with Aloo Gobi and Paneer Skewers (*see* page 142) with Mango Pickle and Minted Mustard Seed & Cucumber Raita (*see* page 194).

1 tbsp ground coriander seeds
2 tbsp ground cumin seeds
6 cardamom seeds
2 tsp fennel seeds
1/2 tsp fenugreek seeds
5cm cinnamon stick, broken up
6 cloves fresh garlic, finely chopped

2 thumbs fresh ginger, finely chopped
2 tsp chilli flakes, or to taste
1 tbsp coriander root and stem, finely chopped
5 tbsp natural yoghurt
2 tbsp vegetable oil

Toast the coriander, cumin, cardamom, fennel and fenugreek seeds with the cinnamon in a heated dry frying pan or skillet, or in a medium oven until just lightly toasted and aromatic. Grind to a coarse powder in your spice grinder or pestle and mortar. Mix with the remaining marinade ingredients. Using disposable gloves, rub the marinade into the lamb. Cover and refrigerate overnight.

2) Cuban-style

- An astonishingly good marinade for lamb or, traditionally at New Year in Cuba, for pork. Serve with Mint Mojo (*see* page 190).

4 tbsp Seville orange marmalade
3 tbsp water
zest of two oranges
2 tbsp oregano, finely chopped
6 cloves fresh garlic, minced
2 tsp cayenne pepper, or to taste
2 tbsp vegetable oil
1 can Coca Cola

Gently heat the marmalade and water together in a pan, stirring until the marmalade has melted. Allow to cool and mix with the orange zest, oregano, garlic, cayenne (if using) and oil. Rub the marinade into the lamb. Place in a strong plastic bag and place the bag in a bowl. Pour the Coca Cola around the meat. Tie the top of the bag securely. If you were simply to place the meat in a bowl, there would not be sufficient Coca Cola to cover the meat, so pouring the can into the bag means that you can massage and turn the meat easily while it is marinating in the fridge.

3) Provençale

- For a fresh clean summery taste, serve with minted new potatoes, chargrilled or wood-roast vegetables and Fresh Green Salsa (*see* page 192) or a tomato-based sauce. As a rule, we don't chop up rosemary, as it can be woody and unpleasant to eat. Bash the sprigs ruthlessly with the back of a heavy knife.
- Infused olive oils are great for marinades and salads and make a great addition to your Top Shelf. They keep well and improve over the weeks. Here we use rosemary oil.
- If you have an abundance of rosemary in your garden, you can produce some rosemary smoke. Soak a large bunch of the herb in water for at least an hour. Towards the end of the grilling process, place the soaked stems on the coals beneath the meat and just smell that aroma.

zest of 3 lemons
4 tbsp rosemary oil (infuse gently warmed olive oil with rosemary sprigs, garlic and peppercorns. Also available from all delis and good supermarkets)
6 cloves garlic, finely chopped
plenty of freshly ground pepper
8-10 sprigs rosemary

Mix together all the ingredients except for the rosemary sprigs. Rub this marinade into the lamb. Bash the rosemary as described above, leaving the leaves on the stem. Tuck around the leg. Refrigerate at least overnight; preferably for two days.

4) Middle Eastern

- The warm spices of the Souk sharpened with lemon and sumac go brilliantly with the sweet savoury flavour of barbecued lamb. This is a thick paste marinade, which will produce a delicious crust on the finished barbecued lamb. Do make an effort to get hold of the pomegranate powder – it adds texture as well as unique flavour to the marinade. Serve Moroccan Lamb with Vivid Green Salad (*see* page 171), Cous Cous Salad (*see* page 161), Blistering Sweet Chilli Sauce (*see* page 187), Green Harissa (*see* page 196) and Middle Eastern Minted Yoghurt (*see* page 196).
- A great idea from Persian cuisine is to serve richly spiced meat, such as this one, with great bunches of fresh herbs. You are invited to nibble on whole stems of fresh herbs between mouthfuls of meat. This acts as a great appetite stimulant, palate cleanser, and anti-oxidant.

4 tsp sumac powder

1 level tsp saffron strands, soaked in 1 tbsp hot water (optional)

2 tbsp pomegranate powder

1 heaped tbsp cumin seeds, ground

1 level tbsp coriander seeds, ground

2 tsp ground cinnamon

3 tsp garlic powder

2 tbsp mild paprika

2 tsp cayenne, or to taste (optional)

good bunch fresh parsley including stalks, chopped
zest of 2 lemons, or 1 finely chopped preserved lemon

4 tbsp natural yoghurt
3 tbsp vegetable oil

Mix together all the ingredients. Rub the marinade into the lamb. Cover and refrigerate overnight.

Lamb Chops with Australian Lemon Myrtle, Garlic and Thyme with Mango, Lime, Red Onion & Mint Salsa

SERVES 6

• 3 hour to overnight marinade

• At Blistering, we have been using lemon myrtle dust on lamb for the last four years. This sensational aromatic Australian herb – with a flavour not a million miles from our own lemon balm, but with less of the aftershave pungency – is better known for its marriage with fish or white meat. Watch out for it in your local deli and try out this magical formula on some spring lamb – it's perfect for cutting through the sweet fattiness of the meat.

12 lamb chops
12 cocktail sticks, soaked for 1 hour (optional)

For the marinade
4 tsp Australian lemon myrtle dust
4 tsp chopped fresh thyme,
6 cloves garlic, finely chopped
1/2 tsp freshly ground black pepper
2 tbsp vegetable oil

For grilling and serving
fine sea salt
Mango Lime, Red Onion & Mint Salsa (*see* page 191)

To prepare the chops Some like lean chops, but others delight in the sweet savouriness of well seasoned lamb fat. Using a sharp knife, trim as desired. For neat presentation of lamb chops and to protect the delicate inner nugget of meat, curl around the fatty tail of the chop and skewer with a soaked cocktail stick to the main body of the meat.

To marinate the chops Combine the marinade ingredients in a bowl and, using disposable gloves, rub it over the chops. Cover and refrigerate overnight or for at least 3 hours.

Before barbecuing Give the chops enough time out of the fridge to lose their chill. Season with salt as desired.

Barbecue Preheat the grill or barbecue sandwich racks to medium-high or 'sizzle' temperature. Clean and lightly oil the rack. Place the chops on the grill and seal for 1-2 minutes on each side. Move to a medium heat and cook for a further 3-5 minutes on each side for a medium-cooked result.

To serve Serve with a spoonful of Mango, Lime, Red Onion and Mint Salsa, new potatoes tossed with butter and parsley and a Vivid Green Salad (*see* page 171).

Tips Try with the Mint Mojo instead (*see* page 190).

Beef:
Whole Sirloin and Whole Beef Fillet and Individual Fillet, Sirloin and Rump Steaks

Cooking a large joint of meat is a very satisfying experience. Eaten inside or outside, everyone loves to see a joint of meat carved at the table. When you cook large joints, remember that people will come back for seconds, so don't carve the joint all in one go, but do so to order. This way, the meat will stay warm and keep its juices. If you are left with any, it'll be great the next day in a sandwich with watercress, tomato, mustard and sea salt.

More readily available in the high street, individual steaks don't need such a long marinating time (although, we would still recommend that you marinate overnight for the full whack of flavour) and can arrive on your guests' plates before they can say *a point s'il vous plait*. We would also strongly recommend that you invest in a set of serrated steak knives.

Choosing your cut of beef When it comes to comparing beef cuts for texture, the basic rule to follow is – the less work the muscle has done during its life, the more tender it will be; the tougher the meat, the longer you can leave it in its marinade. At Blistering, we avoid using large pieces of rump, as it is an awkward shape and can tend to be a little chewy for barbecuing. Individual rump steaks, however, are great.

There are no bones in whole sirloins or fillets, and for fillet in particular, the fat content is pretty low. This makes for a shorter grilling time. These large beef joints are at their best and most tender cooked rare to medium-rare and left to rest for around 15-20 minutes. Beef joints need trimming. So get your butcher to do the following.

To trim sirloin Trim off excess fat and sinew from the bottom of the sirloin, leaving some marbled fat. On the top or skin-side of the piece, there is a layer of fat. If you were to leave this intact, the meat would curl dramatically when placed on the barbecue grill making it almost impossible to cook. To prevent this, trim the fat right back, leaving a strip of fat half the width of the loin. We prefer to cut off the 'chain' (the scraggy tail of meat running under the sirloin). As you have paid for this, you may as well take it home. Stew it up with some kidneys or give it to your dog.

To trim fillet Trim off all sinew leaving the marble fat, which will keep the fillet moist when grilling. Remove the chain, as for the sirloin (above).

The marinating process For a large piece of beef follow the directions for butterflied leg of lamb (*see* page 90).

To Barbecue large pieces of beef
Remove the beef from the fridge half an hour or so before barbecuing to lose its chill. Season all over on both sides with salt and pepper as required.

See directions for the basic principles for barbecuing large pieces of meat in the Butterflied Leg of Lamb instructions (*see* page 90), but see the following paragraphs for grill times for large pieces of sirloin and fillet. As for the lamb, you can use the garlic brine basting technique.

Grill times for a large piece of sirloin
Depending on the thickness of the sirloin,

on a medium heat, a 30-40 minute cooking time, turning every 5-7 minutes should give you a succulent pink medium-cooked result. A temperature probe inserted into the middle of the thickest part of the meat should read 50-55C. Rest the meat for at least 20 minutes, covered with a double layer of tin foil, leaving a small air hole for steam to escape. The air hole is essential to prevent the steam from cooking the beef any further. During the resting process, the sinews relax and absorb the juices. If you were to cut into the meat without resting, juices and blood would stream out of the meat leaving it dry and unappealing.

Grill times for a large piece of fillet

A whole beef fillet tapers to a tail. With a larger fillet, you could just order a cut from the thick end, but if you do have a tapering piece of meat, you will have to be careful not to overcook the thinner end. At Blistering, we often find this is convenient to cater for the more squeamish guest who prefers a better-cooked piece of meat. We do however tend to position the meat on the grill, so that the thinner tail end is over a cooler area, usually towards the edge of the barbecue grill, making for slower grilling. If the thinner end is cooking too fast, you can place a double sheet of foil under this part of the fillet to slow the cooking down.

Depending on the thickness of the fillet, on a low-medium heat, 20-25 minutes should give you a succulent pink medium-cooked result. A temperature probe inserted into the middle of the thickest part of the meat should read 50-55C. Rest the meat for at least 10-15 minutes, covered with a double layer of tin foil, leaving a small air hole for steam to escape as for sirloin (above).

Beef Marinades

Blistering's most popular beef marinades tend to be punchier than some used for other meats, birds or fish. This isn't to say that you shouldn't use them elsewhere, but if you do so, use with care, reduce quantities and shorten the marinating time. On the flipside, you can apply any number of other marinades to beef – just flick through the rest of the book.

You don't need to marinate beef steaks for as long as the larger pieces, though overnight does give the best flavour. The larger pieces really do benefit from an overnight marinade.

All marinade quantities will flavour a 1.7 kg piece of sirloin or fillet, or a similar weight in pre-cut individual steaks. This will be plenty for 8 guests.

To Marinate and Barbecue Individual Steaks

Individual steaks need to be marinated for at least three hours, though to achieve thorough flavouring, overnight is best. Remove the steaks from the fridge half an hour or so before barbecuing to lose the chill of the fridge. Shake off any excess marinade. Season on both sides as required.

It's important that your grill bars are brushed clean and lightly oiled, as described above for the larger joints, to prevent sticking of individual steaks. The grill must be heated to medium high or 'sizzle' temperature. The steaks will make a 'tzshhhsssssss' noise when they are placed on the rack. After cooking, the resting process is as essential as it is for the larger pieces of meat. For ideal resting, use a warmed metal baking tray or plate and cover the meat with perforated foil to stop your meat from cooling down before serving.

The following cook times are approximate. Times vary depending on how thick your steak is. Experience is the only sure thing to depend on.

Blue On a hot grill, seal on each side for one minute.
Rare Continue to cook for a further 2-3 minutes on each side, resting for 3-4 minutes.
Medium Continue to cook for a further 1-2 minutes on each side, resting for 3-4 minutes
Well done Continue to cook for a further 2-3 minutes on each side, resting for 3-4 minutes

1) Devilled Beef

• Inspired by old English recipes for preserving meat long after the kill, devilling is a great way to set off beef. Serve with buttery baked potatoes and a green leaf salad. If you like it spicy, increase the cayenne pepper.

1 tbsp English mustard
4 tbsp wholegrain French mustard
1 tsp ground allspice
6 tbsp Worcestershire Sauce
4 tbsp honey
2 tbsp hot horseradish
2 tsp cayenne pepper

3 tbsp vegetable oil
150 ml strong stout

Blend all the above. Place the meat in a strong plastic bag and place the bag in a bowl. Pour the marinade around the meat. Tie the top of the bag securely and massage to ensure all surfaces are coated. Using the bag-in-a-bowl technique, you can easily turn the meat during the marinating process. Refrigerate overnight for larger pieces of meat, and for at least 3 hours for individual steaks (though we would recommend an overnight soak for all beef for full flavour).

2) Thai Hot and Sour

• Inspired by our love for classic salty, sweet, spicy, sour Thai Beef Salad. If you can get hold of Thai basil, it adds a terrific sharp aniseed flavour. Great served with the Thai Salad (see page166) and steamed rice or a simple rice salad.

4 tbsp rice vinegar
110g palm sugar or light brown sugar
6 stems lemon grass, chopped into 5 cm pieces and bashed with the back of a knife
10 lime leaves, torn in two
6 tbsp tomato ketchup
4 tbsp sesame oil
2-3 tsp red chilli flakes, or to taste
100g fresh ginger, finely chopped
zest of 3 limes
8 tbsp fish sauce

1 large bunch coriander, including stalks and roots, finely chopped
1 tbsp chopped Thai basil (optional)

Place the rice vinegar, palm sugar, lemon grass and lime leaves in a pan and heat gently until the sugar is dissolved. Bring to the boil and remove from the heat. Add all the other ingredients except for the coriander and basil, which should be added once the mixture has cooled. Using disposable gloves, rub the marinade into the beef. Cover and refrigerate overnight for larger pieces of meat, and for at least 3 hours for individual steaks (though we would recommend an overnight soak for all beef for full flavour).

3) Bourguignon

• Marinating in wine imparts delicious flavour and transforms the texture of the meat. This is particularly fantastic for the more robust sirloins – and even for rumps if you choose. For a classic bourguignon effect, serve with seasoned barbecued field mushrooms and shallots. Make up a Bearnaise Sauce (see page 180) and you're in barbecue heaven.

300ml bottle of port
1 x 75cl bottle red wine
2 bay leaves, torn
450g shallots, halved lengthways
8 cloves garlic, peeled and chopped
1 level tbsp chopped fresh sage
1 level tbsp chopped fresh tarragon
1 tbsp cracked black pepper

vegetable oil for light brushing of meat

Bring the port and wine to the boil in a pan with the bay leaves. Simmer until reduced by half. Take off the heat and leave to cool. Add the shallots, garlic and herbs.

Rub the meat with the pepper and place in a strong plastic bag. After the marinade has cooled completely, place the bagged beef in a bowl, and pour the marinade around the meat. Tie the top of the bag securely. If you were simply to place the meat in a bowl, there would not be sufficient marinade to cover the meat, so pouring the marinade into the bag means that you can massage and turn the meat easily while it is in the fridge. Refrigerate overnight. Since the marinade does not contain oil, the meat must be lightly oiled to prevent sticking during the barbecuing process. So after marinating, drain the meat and pat it dry with kitchen paper. Lightly brush all surfaces of the joint or individual steaks with vegetable oil.

• It would be a crime to throw away the marinade, so try this fantastic **Bourguignon Sauce**.

strained bourguignon marinade
50g chilled butter, cut into small pieces
sea salt and freshly ground black pepper

Pour the strained marinade into a non-reactive saucepan and place over a medium to high heat. Bring to the boil, skimming off any scum and reduce to a quarter of its original volume. Take off the heat. Hold back on the final stage of adding the butter until after you have barbecued your beef, as the finished sauce does not hold well. Adding one small piece of butter at a time, whisk to thicken and emulsify your sauce. You will end up with a rich glossy sauce.

Tips Save the shallots from the marinade. Skewer, brush with a little oil and season well with salt and pepper. Barbecue on medium heat until coloured and softened (10-12 minutes).

4) Hong Kong Style

• This is beef served with horseradish in an oriental guise – though as anyone who has popped a dollop in their mouth by accident will know, wasabi is horseradish with the lurid green volume turned up. Serve with Sweet and Sour Slaw (*see* page 168), Egg Noodle Salad with Sugar Snaps (*see* page 162) and Wasabi Mayonnaise (*see* page 178).

1 tbsp Szechwan peppercorns
1 tbsp Chinese five spice
1 tsp dried chilli flakes, or to taste
300ml Mirin (Chinese rice wine)
110g palm sugar or soft brown sugar
300ml light soy sauce
3 tbsp oyster sauce
2 tbsp tomato purée

vegetable oil for light brushing of meat

Toast the Szechwan pepper in a dry skillet or frying pan for one minute, or until aromatic. Grind in a spice grinder or pestle and mortar. Add to Chinese five spice and chilli flakes.

Rub the mixture over the beef. Place in a strong plastic bag.

In a saucepan, heat the Mirin gently with the palm sugar. Once the sugar has dissolved, bring to the boil and flame the Mirin to cook off the alcohol. Remove from the heat and add the soy, oyster sauce and tomato purée, whisking to get rid of any lumps of tomato purée. Allow to cool before pouring around the beef in its bag. Tie the top of the bag securely. Refrigerate overnight or for at least 3 hours. Turn the bag a few times to expose all sides of the meat to the marinade.

Since the marinade does not contain oil, the meat must be lightly oiled to prevent sticking during the barbecuing process. So after marinating, drain the meat and pat it dry with kitchen paper. Lightly brush all surfaces of the joint or individual steaks with vegetable oil.

When the marinating time is up, pour off the marinade, boil it up for 7 minutes and use it either as a sauce for the meat, or as a baste during the barbecuing process.

T-bone Steak with Garlic Parsley Butter

SERVES 6

- A firm favourite with our American friends, the enormous T-bone steak is thick and juicy and, being large and flat-cut, marvellously easy to barbecue. You'll need big plates and steak knives. Serve it with Cajun Sweet Potato Chips (see page 30), a green leaf salad and the garlic parsley butter.
- At Blistering, we don't believe in placing cold butter on your hot steaks. We melt the butter with the garlic to allow the flavours to blend and infuse. Adding the parsley at the last minute, we pour the butter over the steaks before resting to allow the juices to balance and flavours to meld. Unbeatable.

6 x 350g T-bone steaks
vegetable oil for brushing
fine sea salt and freshly ground black pepper
175g salted butter
3 cloves garlic, finely chopped
a good handful of English parsley, finely chopped

Brush the T-bones lightly with vegetable oil (don't use butter, as it has a lower flash point than oil and will burn). Season both sides well with salt and pepper.

Place the butter and garlic in a heavy-bottomed pan and place this on the edge of the barbecue, or if you have the facility, on a higher rack to melt and cook on a low heat while you barbecue the T-bones.

Barbecue Preheat the grill to medium–high or 'sizzle' temperature. Clean and lightly oil the rack. Seal both sides for 1–2 minutes and then follow the approximate timings for steaks on page 98.

To serve Remove the steaks from the barbecue to a warmed oven tray. Pour over the garlic parsley butter, cover with a double layer of foil, remembering to leave a hole for steam to escape and leave to rest for 5 minutes allowing time for the muscles to relax and for the garlic and parsley butter to infuse.

Tips It isn't easy for a beginner to achieve the perfect 'doneness' of a steak. A temperature probe is of little use for these thinner cuts of meat, so give the steak a prod with your finger. If it gives fleshy resistance, like the ball of your hand, then it's still pretty raw. Alternatively, using a small pointed knife, poke it into the fattest point near the bone to see how bloody the flesh is.

Flat-out T-bones are marvellously easy to barbecue.

Minute Steaks with Green Peppercorn and Chive Butter

SERVES 6

- The simplest barbecue dish on the planet. You just can't go wrong and it's delicious: we had to sneak it in. The best cut for the job is sirloin steak, with a small amount of fat on its back. Grill one steak per guest at a time, as it is so quick to grill and is best eaten straight away. The inevitable request for a second should come soon after.
- Serve with shoestring chips, garlicky beef tomato salad with Buffalo Mozzarella, lemon-dressed rocket leaves and a glass of Provence rosé.

12 x 100g pieces of sirloin, well trimmed
vegetable oil for brushing
fine sea salt and freshly ground black pepper
100g salted butter
1 heaped tsp bottled green peppercorns in brine, drained and crushed
3 tbsp chives, finely chopped

Place one of the steaks between two pieces of Clingfilm on a chopping board. Bash out lightly with a meat hammer or rolling pin to a thickness of about 5mm, giving a flat steak measuring around 7 x 15cm. Brush lightly with vegetable oil. Season both sides with salt and pepper. Repeat with the remaining steaks.

Place the butter and green peppercorns in a heavy-bottomed pan and place this on the edge of the barbecue, or if you have the facility, on a higher rack to melt and cook on a low heat while you barbecue the steaks. Add the chives to the green peppercorn butter a few minutes before pouring it over the meat.

Barbecue Preheat the grill to medium–high or 'sizzle' temperature. Clean and lightly oil the rack. A total of a minute or two's grilling on each side should give you a medium-rare steak.

To serve Remove the steaks from the barbecue to warmed plates and spoon over the Peppercorn and Chive Butter. These steaks are so thin and tender that you should serve them straight away without any resting beyond the time it takes for your guests to help themselves to fries and salads.

Tips You should also try this recipe with veal steaks, duck breast or pork tenderloin bashed out in the same way.

Nirvana on a Summer's day.

Tangy Cranberry Pork Chops

SERVES 6

- 3 hour to overnight marinade
- If it ain't broke, don't fix it. Since pork and fruit go together so well, why break the tradition?
- Serve with buttery baked potatoes and Crunchy Carrot Salad (see page 170).

6 large pork chops

For the marinade
4 cloves garlic, finely chopped
2 tbsp chopped fresh marjoram or oregano
2 tbsp vegetable oil
zest of 2 oranges
$1/2$ tsp freshly ground black pepper
6 bay leaves, each torn in two pieces

For grilling, basting and for the table
sea salt
300ml Cranberry & Orange Sauce (see page 184)

To prepare the pork chops Trim off excess fat from the chops. Place on a meat board and, using a sharp knife, cut through the remaining fat at approximately 2.5cm intervals. This will stop the chops from curling up at the edges during grilling and so allow for more even cooking.

To marinate the chops Mix together the marinade ingredients, excluding the bay leaves, in a large bowl. Using disposable gloves, place the chops one at a time in the bowl and rub the marinade over both sides of the chops. Place a torn bay leaf onto each chop, wrap tightly together on a plate with Clingfilm, or pack into a plastic bag and refrigerate overnight or for at least 3 hours.

Before barbecuing Give the chops enough time out of the fridge to lose their chill. Season well with salt as required.

Barbecue Preheat the grill to medium-high or 'sizzle' temperature. Clean and lightly oil the rack. Grill the chops for 2 minutes on each side to seal the meat. Move to a cooler, medium hot, part of the barbecue. Spread 2 heaped teaspoons of Cranberry & Orange Sauce over one side of the chop and place this chop on the grill, sauce-side down. Repeat with the other five and grill for 5-7 minutes. Spread 2 heaped teaspoons of the sauce on the top side of each chop. Turn and grill for 5-7 minutes on this other side. It's famously important for pork to be cooked through, but overcooking produces dried-out leather. Test for 'doneness' around the bone using a small sharply pointed knife.

To serve Remove the chops from the barbecue to a warmed oven tray. Allow to rest for 4-5 minutes covered with a double layer of foil, remembering to leave a hole for steam to escape. Serve with more Cranberry & Orange Sauce.

Pork and fruit – the perfect combination, and even better on the barbecue with maximum caramelisation.

Spanish Pork with Oregano, Chorizo and Rich Red Pepper Sauce

SERVES 6

- 3 hour to overnight marinade

- The authentic rich cooked-in Spanish flavours of this recipe make for a great one-pot Autumn dish. This is a great way to use the barbecue – adding barbecued ingredients to an ovenproof dish, which sits on the barbecue, continuing the cooking process. You can make the sauce up a day or two ahead.
- There are as many types of chorizo sausage as there are days of the year. For this recipe search out the softer 'cooking' or 'frying' chorizo (*see* Suppliers' appendix, page 215).

1 kg pork leg meat, trimmed and cut into 3cm dice
4-5 x 30cm metal skewers, or equivalent

For the pork marinade
2 tbsp mild paprika
2 tsp garlic powder or granules
3 tsp dried oregano
1/2 tsp freshly ground black pepper
80ml Madeira wine, or sweet sherry
80ml apple juice
2 tbsp olive oil

For the sauce
2 tbsp olive oil
1 medium onion, finely chopped
4 cloves garlic, finely chopped
2 red peppers, finely chopped
2 glasses red wine
1 bay leaf

1 x 400g tin chopped tomatoes
2 anchovy fillets, finely chopped
1/2 tsp celery salt
1 tsp sugar
2 heaped tbsp stoned good quality black olives
sea salt and freshly ground black pepper

For grilling and serving
350g good quality chorizo 'frying' or 'cooking'
   sausage
olive oil for brushing
fine sea salt

1 tbsp freshly chopped oregano

To marinate the pork Mix together the marinade ingredients in a jug. Place the pork in a strong plastic bag and pour the marinade around the meat. Tie the top and give it a good massage. Refrigerate preferably overnight, but for at least 3 hours.

To make the sauce Heat the olive oil in a heavy-bottomed saucepan. Add the onion and garlic and cook on medium for 2-3 minutes, stirring to prevent sticking. Add the red peppers and continue to cook for 5 minutes or so, or until the peppers soften. Turn up the heat and add the red wine and bay leaf. Simmer to reduce the wine down to half its volume. Add the remaining ingredients and continue to cook on a low heat for 20 minutes or so to cook out the tomatoes and meld together the flavours. If the sauce becomes too thick, add a little water. Season to taste with salt and pepper.

Final preparation If they are in a chain, delink the chorizo sausages. Before barbecuing, give the pork and chorizo enough time out of the fridge to lose their chill. Drain the pork of marinade and thread onto metal skewers, brush with oil and season with salt as required. Pour the pepper sauce into an ovenproof dish (e.g. terracotta, earthenware, Le Creuset) and place onto a cool part of the barbecue or into the wood-fired oven to barely simmer, adding water if the sauce is drying out.

Barbecue Preheat the grill to medium–high or 'sizzle' temperature. Clean and lightly oil the rack. Grill the chorizo sausages for 4–5 minutes, turning as they seal and colour on all sides. You don't want the chorizo to

lose its delicious fat into the coals. Remove the sausages from the grill to a chopping board. Slice into 1-inch lengths and throw into the sauce to continue to cook and stew on a cooler part of the barbecue – or if you have one, pop it in the wood-fired oven. You should cook the chorizo in the simmering sauce for at least a further 15 minutes. Don't let the sauce dry out – add a little hot water if necessary. Grill the pork skewers, sealing on all sides for 3-4 minutes. Move to a medium heat and continue to grill for a further 10-12 minutes, turning every 2-3 minutes, or until cooked through.

To serve Slide the grilled pork off the skewers onto the chorizo pepper sauce. Stir a little to coat the pork. Scatter with fresh oregano and serve with pasta or wood-roasted potatoes, a crunchy leaf salad and a glass of rustic Spanish red. You should serve the dish pretty swiftly, as the pork will not benefit from stewing and it will begin to dry out.

Tips The sauce is terrific as a base sauce for a pizza. It also freezes well. If using the wood-fired oven to cook the sauce, try baking some baby potatoes tossed in olive oil and sea salt to serve alongside.

Jerked Rack of Ribs with a Rum, Pineapple and Mango Glaze

SERVES 6

- 3 hour to overnight marinade

- Jerked Ribs are to the Caribbean what Fish and Chips are to the UK. We've added a Sweet and Sour Pineapple Glaze, so you will need finger bowls and reams of napkins.
- WARNING: We use a scotch bonnet chilli here. While handling these, we firmly advise the use of disposable gloves. Or, if you do use your bare hands, do not touch any sensitive body areas after chopping.

2.25 kg racks of pork ribs

The cooking liquor
1 onion, peeled and roughly chopped
4 cloves garlic, peeled and roughly chopped
2 sticks celery, roughly chopped
3 cloves
2 bay leaves
2 tsp dried thyme
$1/2$ tsp freshly ground black pepper

For the marinade
2 bunches spring onions, washed, dried, trimmed
   and roughly chopped
2 tbsp mild paprika
1 scotch bonnet chilli (see warning above) or
   3 bird's eye chillies, finely chopped – leave seeds

in for extra heat
1 heaped tsp ground cinnamon
$1/4$ tsp freshly ground nutmeg
2 tsp celery salt
1 tbsp chopped fresh thyme
$1/2$ tsp freshly ground black pepper
2 tbsp red wine vinegar
4 tbsp vegetable oil
2 tbsp soy sauce

For the glaze
140ml rum
400ml pineapple juice
4 tbsp honey
4 tbsp red wine vinegar
1 tbsp smooth mango chutney

For grilling
sea salt

To poach the ribs Place the rack of ribs in a large pan and cover with cold water. If you don't have a pan large enough for the ribs, cut the racks into two or three pieces. Add all the cooking liquor ingredients. Bring to the boil and skim off the froth. Simmer for 35-40 minutes, skimming as the froth or scum develops. When you can see the meat peeling away from the top of the rib bones, take the pan off the heat and allow the ribs to cool down in the liquor.

To marinate the ribs Pulse the spring onions in a blender. Add all the other marinade ingredients and pulse again. Drain the still-warm ribs and flick off any bits of cooking liquor debris. Place the ribs in a bowl and coat thoroughly on both sides with the marinade. Using disposable gloves, massage the marinade all over the surfaces of the meat. Cover and leave to marinate for at least 3 hours or overnight.

For the glaze Heat the rum in a heavy bottomed stainless steel pan. Let it ignite to burn off the alcohol. Add the other ingredients, turn up the heat and reduce the volume by half or to a thick syrup.

Before barbecuing Give the ribs enough time out of the fridge to lose their chill. Season with salt as required.

Barbecue Preheat the barbecue grill to medium or 'cook' temperature. Clean and lightly oil the rack. The ribs are already cooked, so in this barbecuing process, you are browning the outside and heating the meat through to the middle, while retaining the moisture. Place the ribs on the grill and cook for 15-20 minutes, basting the ribs with the glaze and turning every 4-5 minutes.

To serve Serve from a large wooden chopping board with classic Jamaican Rice and Peas (*see* page 160) and Creole Slaw (*see* page 172).

Tips For a good old US BBQ Rack of Ribs, omit the chilli and cloves from the cooking liquor and use the Blistering Sweet and Sticky Barbecue Sauce (*see* page 184) for both the marinade and glaze.

Venison Steak with Sloe Gin, Juniper and Thyme

SERVES 6

- 3 hour to overnight marinade

- This is a classic Burn's Night dish, or delicious on any Autumn evening when venison and roots are well in season and last year's batch of sloe gin is ready for opening. Don't waste the marinade – transform it into a delicious rich Sloe Gin Butter Sauce.

6 x 175g venison fillet steaks

For the marinade and sauce
10 juniper berries
3 cloves garlic, finely chopped
100g shallots, finely chopped
1 tbsp freshly chopped thyme leaves
1/2 tsp freshly ground pepper
200ml Sloe gin
200ml good red wine

Additional ingredients for the Sloe Gin Butter Sauce
200ml good red wine
50g chilled butter, cut into small pieces
sea salt

For grilling and serving
olive oil for brushing
sea salt

To marinate the venison Toast the juniper berries in a heated dry frying pan or skillet, shaking to prevent burning, until just lightly toasted and aromatic. Blitz to a coarse powder in your spice grinder or grind in a pestle and mortar. In a small bowl, mix the ground juniper with the garlic, shallots, thyme leaves and pepper. Place your steaks on a plate or tray and sprinkle the dry marinade evenly over both sides of the meat. Transfer the steaks to a strong plastic bag. Place the bag in a bowl and pour the sloe gin and red wine around the meat. Tie the top and give it a good massage. Refrigerate overnight or for at least 3 hours.

Drain the marinade off the venison steaks and brush off and discard any stray bits of shallot. Pat the steaks dry with kitchen paper and brush lightly with olive oil. Season with salt as desired.

To make the sauce Pour the strained marinade into a small saucepan. Add the extra 200ml of red wine. Place over a medium to high heat, bring to the boil, skimming off any scum and reduce to a quarter of the volume. Take off the heat. Hold back on the final stage of adding the butter until after you have barbecued your venison steaks, as the finished sauce does not hold well. When you are ready to serve, heat up the reduction and adding one small piece of butter at a time, whisk to thicken and emulsify the sauce. Season to taste.

Barbecue Preheat the grill to medium–high or 'sizzle' temperature. Be sure that the grill is cleaned and lightly oiled (*see* barbecue instructions for Minute Steak on page 104). Place the steaks on the grill and seal for 1-2 minutes on each side. Move to a medium heat and cook for a further 2-4 minutes on each side. Grill-times vary widely depending on the thickness of the cut. Note that venison fillet steaks are at their best cooked medium: overcooked, they become dry and grainy.

Final preparation Remove the steaks from the barbecue to a warmed tray. Allow to rest for 3-4 minutes covered with a double layer of foil, remembering to leave a hole for steam to escape. In the meantime, finish the sauce as described above.

To serve Serve individual steaks with a spoonful of the sauce. If you have a wood-fired oven, rustle up some Wood-roast Potatoes (*see* page 157) and Autumnal Wood-roast Vegetables (*see* page 150).

Tips To make it a 'real McCoy' Burn's Night, boil up a haggis too – great with any apple or Cumberland sauce.

If you don't want to make the Sloe Gin Butter Sauce, use Red Onion Confit (*see* page 194).

Peppered Ostrich Steaks with a Pastrami Spice Rub with Mango, Papaya & Passion Fruit Salsa

SERVES 6

- 3 hour to overnight marinade

- This pastrami rub is a great mix to make up and keep in an airtight jar on your Top Shelf.
- Ostrich steaks are lean and slightly gamy, with the flavour and texture of fillet steak. They are best cooked rare to medium rare.
- The Pastrami Rub includes using the choice of Garlic Powder or Garlic Granules. The mellower Garlic Powder is a great product and is available in Asian Stores. You'll find the stronger Garlic Granules on the supermarket spice shelves. If you can't find either, then just add finely chopped fresh garlic to taste.

6 x 175g ostrich steaks

The Pastrami Rub (fits in a 454g jam jar)
1 1/2 tbsp coriander seeds
3 tsp black mustard seeds
1 tbsp yellow mustard seeds
2 tsp dried green or white peppercorns (optional)
1 tbsp black peppercorns
1 tbsp garlic powder or 2 tsp garlic granules
3 tsp dried thyme
2 tbsp dark brown sugar
3 tbsp paprika

For grilling and serving
2 tbsp vegetable oil
fine sea salt

For the Pastrami Rub Toast the coriander seeds in a heated dry frying pan or skillet, shaking to prevent catching, until just lightly toasted and aromatic. Coarsely grind the coriander, mustard seeds and peppercorns in a spice grinder. Take care not to over-grind, as you don't want to produce a powder. In a small bowl, combine the ground ingredients with all the other ingredients. Store in an airtight jar.

To marinate your ostrich Massage the Pastrami Rub generously over the surface of the meat – about a heaped teaspoon for each steak. Refrigerate overnight or for at least 3 hours.

Before barbecuing Give the steaks enough time out of the fridge to lose their chill. Season with salt as desired.

Barbecue Preheat the grill to medium–high or 'sizzle' temperature. Clean and lightly oil the rack. Place the steaks on the grill and seal for 1–2 minutes on each side. Move to a medium heat and cook for a further 2–3 minutes on each side. Grill-times vary widely depending on the thickness of the cut. Note that ostrich steaks are at their best cooked medium–rare: if you overcook them they become dry and grainy.

To serve Serve individual steaks topped with a spoonful of the Mango, Papaya & Passion Fruit Salsa (*see* page 191), New and Sweet Potato Salad (*see* page 156) and dressed mixed leaves.

A great alternative to traditional peppered steak.

FISH AND SHELLFISH

Barbecuing Whole Fish

How many beachside restaurants have we found ourselves in revelling in wood-fired or barbecued fish served with delicious salads, piles of steaming rice or hunks of bread? In Turkey, in India, Thailand, Sri Lanka, Australia. A whole fish on the bone, big enough to share, with a delicious marinade, served with an inspiring salad, bread and a bottle of crisp chilled wine is as good as it gets.

When it comes to barbecuing, whole fish on the bone has many advantages over fish fillets or steaks. The skin acts to protect the delicate flesh from the direct heat, giving a succulent result. A whole fish is less likely to stick to the grill and holds together perfectly, making it much easier to handle. Whole fish also bring more drama to the table and being a communal dish, bring people together – as long as they don't mind getting their fingers sticky.

When barbecuing a fish, bear in mind that the flesh will continue to cook for a few minutes after it is removed from the grill. Do beware of overcooking, as overcooked, dried, flavourless fish is as disappointing as succulent perfectly cooked fish is delicious.

Sardines and mackerel are made for the barbecue having a good natural oil content. Blistering favourites include grouper, small tuna, gilt-head bream, sea bass and snapper. You don't have to do much, but whatever you do make sure that your barbecue grill is really clean and lightly oiled. Make your life easy and get your fishmonger to gut, scale and trim all the fins from your fish. Slash the skin a few times, season, oil and grill... or try one of the following recipes.

Whole fish bring drama to the grill, with myriad advantages over fish fillets or steaks.

Whole Gilthead Bream with Lemon, Garlic and Parsley served with Caper Butter

SERVES 6

- 2 hour marinade, or overnight is fine

- A great sized fish for one person of good appetite, it has a similar flavour to, but a firmer texture than sea bass and the flesh falls very easily off the bone. The 450g fish used in this recipe grills at the perfect rate to produce a crispy skin, while cooking the flesh through for a perfectly moist result. If you are barbecuing larger fish you would need to use the foil and banana leaf method described in the red snapper recipe on page 118. A sandwich rack comes in here, as it's so easy to turn the fish.
- This timeless marinade could be applied to any fish on the planet.

6 x 450g gilthead bream or sea bream

The marinade
4 tbsp olive oil
6 cloves garlic, finely chopped
zest of 3 lemons
6 level tbsp chopped parsley
$1/2$ tsp ground black pepper

To serve
175g unsalted butter
$1^1/2$ level tbsp capers (baby if possible), washed well
fine sea salt
3 lemons, cut into wedges

To prepare and marinate the fish Have your fishmonger scale, gut and remove the fins from your fish. Using a sharp knife, score the bream on the diagonal three or four times on each side through the skin, about $1/2$cm into the flesh. In a large bowl, combine the olive oil with the garlic, lemon zest, 4 tbsp of the parsley and the pepper.

Rub this marinade over the fish, into the cuts and inside the cavity. Cover and refrigerate for at least 2 hours. Overnight is fine but unnecessary. Place the butter and capers in a small non-reactive saucepan and leave to melt on the edge of the barbecue, or if you have the facility, on a higher rack to melt on a low heat while you barbecue the fish. Season the fish well on both sides with salt.

Barbecue Preheat the hinged sandwich rack or barbecue grill to medium-high or 'sizzle' temperature. Clean and lightly oil the rack. If using a hinged sandwich rack, be careful not to squash the fish, as you don't want to damage the delicate flesh while grilling. Place the fish on the heat and cook for 5-7 minutes on the first side. If the coals are too hot, rake them away slightly, adjust the height of your grill or pop a lid over the fish to slow down the heat.

If using a sandwich rack, turn the rack and continue to grill for a further 5-7 minutes on the other side or until the skin is crisp and the flesh just cooked through.

If grilling directly on the barbecue grill, do not attempt to move the fish until its skin is crisping, otherwise it will stick. Use a fish slice to gently turn the fish over. Grill for a further 5-7 minutes or until cooked through. To test for doneness either use your temperature probe (reading around 60C when cooked), or have a peep inside the flesh, piercing it at its thickest point with a small sharp knife.

To serve Transfer the fish to a warmed serving plate or individual plates. Stir the remaining 2 tbsp of the chopped parsley into the warmed caper butter and spoon generously over the fish. Serve with plenty of lemon wedges, Grilled Fennel with Beef Tomatoes, Fresh Mozzarella, Salmariglio (*see* page 146) and warm bread. Alternatively, serve Turkish style with Aubergines and Creamy Garlic Yoghurt (*see* page 148).

Tips We would advise the use of a bones bowl, warm lemon-water finger bowls and paper napkins.

Whole Sea Bass with Fennel Dill Butter

SERVES 6

- 2 hour marinade
- Not cheap, but a great treat once in a while, particularly with this delicious, incredibly simple sauce.
- If you can get your hands on the more delicate baby fennel, all the better.

6 x 450g or 3 x 900g sea bass
approximately 3 tbsp olive oil
3 tsp fennel seeds, ground
6 bay leaves
fine sea salt and freshly ground black pepper
175g unsalted butter
2 medium fennel bulbs, or 6 baby fennel, cored and finely sliced
juice of 2 lemons
3 tbsp chopped dill

To prepare the fish Have your fishmonger scale, gut and remove the fins from your fish. Score the bass two or three times on each side through the skin, about $^{1}/_{2}$ cm into the flesh. Brush the outside of the fish with some of the olive oil. Dust the cavity of the fish with half of the ground fennel seeds, sprinkling the remaining half evenly over the outer skin. Scrunch up the bay leaves and place one in each fish cavity. Cover and refrigerate for 2 hours, or overnight will do no harm.

Before barbecuing Give the fish enough time out of the fridge to lose their chill. Season well inside and out with salt and pepper.

Melt and heat up 50g of the butter in a saucepan. Add the fennel, season with salt and pepper and cook gently, stirring, for 8-10 minutes, or until well softened. Add the lemon juice and continue to cook for 5-7 minutes or until softened. Add the rest of the butter, melt it and adjust the seasoning as desired. Leave on the side of the barbecue to stew.

Barbecue Preheat the hinged sandwich rack or barbecue grill to medium-high or 'sizzle' temperature. Clean and lightly oil the rack. *See* barbecue instructions for Gilthead Bream on page 115.

To serve Stir the dill into the warm fennel butter. Transfer the fish to a large serving platter and pour the butter over the fish. Serve simply with some minted new potatoes and French beans.

A recipe as simple as it is impressive.

Mackerel with Lemon and Herbs and Brown Bread and Butter

SERVES 6

- Barbecued mackerel is princely, extremely tasty and best served simply. Maybe one day like monkfish, scallops and oysters, it will be the turn of the mackerel to be in great demand and command a high price in the market. Until then, take advantage of its great value and availability.
- Mackerel is an oily fish, so is perfect for the barbecue. We prefer to serve it with lemon wedges, roasted ripe tomatoes scattered with garden herbs and brown bread and butter.

6 x 450g mackerel

To grill and serve
vegetable oil
fine sea salt and freshly ground black pepper
2 lemons, each cut into 6 wedges
picked garden herb leaves as available
  – parsley, tarragon, chervil, sweet cicely,
  chives, dill, fennel

To prepare the fish Have your fishmonger gut your mackerel and remove the fins. Using a sharp knife, score the fish two or three times on each side through the skin, about $1/2$ cm into the flesh. Although mackerel is an oily fish, it does have a very delicate skin, so brush it lightly with vegetable oil before placing on the grill. Season well with salt and pepper.

Barbecue Preheat the barbecue to medium-high, or 'sizzle' temperature. Clean and lightly oil the rack. *See* barbecue instructions for Gilthead Bream on page 115.

To serve Scatter the barbecued fish with fresh picked garden herb leaves and served with lemon wedges, stacks of buttered brown bread and a tray of well-roasted tomatoes. It may be as well to provide a plate for bones.

Tips Catch your own mackerel and grill them straight away on the beach. There's nothing better.

Simple and delicious – and all the better if you've caught it yourself.

Red Snapper Thai Style

SERVES 6

- 2 hour marinade, or overnight is fine

6 x 500g red snapper

For the marinade
2 tbsp vegetable oil
3 stems lemon grass, finely sliced on an angle
6 lime leaves, finely shredded
2-3 large red chillies, or to taste, finely sliced on an angle
1 thumb ginger, peeled and finely chopped
1 tbsp palm sugar or soft brown sugar
6 tbsp chopped coriander
2 tbsp fish sauce (nam pla)
2 tbsp vegetable oil for brushing
sea salt

To serve
3 limes, halved

To prepare and marinate the fish Have your fishmonger scale, gut and trim the fins of your fish. Using a sharp knife, score the snapper on the diagonal three or four times on each side through the skin, about $1/2$cm into the flesh. Heat the oil in a heavy-bottomed pan. Add the lemon grass, lime leaves, chillies and ginger and cook gently for 2 minutes to soften and bring out the flavours. Melt in the sugar and allow to cool. Add the coriander and fish sauce. Rub this marinade over the fish, into the cuts and inside the cavity. Cover and refrigerate for at least 2 hours. Overnight is fine but unnecessary. Brush all over the surface of the fish with the oil. Season well on both sides with salt.

Barbecue Preheat the hinged sandwich rack or barbecue grill to medium-high or 'sizzle' temperature. Clean and lightly oil the rack. *See* barbecue instructions for Gilthead Bream on p115.

To serve Transfer the fish to a warmed serving plate or individual plates. Serve with sliced limes, Plantain and Onion Skewers (*see* page 144) and Garlic Yoghurt Sauce (*see* page 181).

This fish is great on the barbecue; its flesh is firm, meaty and sweet, and stands up brilliantly to the strong flavours of Thailand.

Jamaican Whole Red Snapper stuffed with Curry Butter wrapped in Banana Leaves

SERVES 6

- 2 hour marinade, or overnight is fine

- The bigger the fish the better for this one. Try and order one fish that will be big enough for 6 people. The banana leaf wrap helps to protect and keep the fish beautifully moist.
- Scotch bonnet peppers are the traditional Jamaican chilli, but as they are perilously hot, they are not to everyone's taste. If you are up to it, use them, but here we use the more lily-livered large red chillies available widely in supermarkets.

1 x 3kg red snapper or equivalent weight of smaller fish

For the curry butter
225g unsalted butter, softened
1½ tbsp mild curry powder
1 tbsp curry leaves, chopped
2 thumbs ginger, peeled and finely chopped
1 level tsp ground allspice
3 large red chillies, sliced into rings
3 tbsp chopped fresh coriander
1½ tsp salt and plenty of freshly ground black pepper

To grill
1 large banana leaf, and extra strong turkey foil

To serve
3 limes, cut into wedges

To prepare and stuff the fish Have your fishmonger scale, gut and remove the fins from your fish. Score the snapper three or four times on each side through the skin, about 1cm into the large fish, or a little less if using smaller fish. Cream the butter in a large bowl with a wooden spoon, or use a food mixer fitted with the cake beater. Add all the other ingredients and mix well. Spoon two-thirds of the curry butter into the cavity of the fish and spread the remainder on both sides of the fish working the butter into the cuts.

To wrap the fish Wipe the banana leaf clean with a damp cloth. To make the banana leaf more flexible and so easier to work with, hold it 5–7cm above a naked flame and warm it up all over for 10–12 seconds. Wrap the banana leaf around the fish, leaving the head uncovered. If you can't get hold of banana leaves, be sure to oil the foil well. Tear two pieces of strong foil at least 20cm longer than the fish and place them on top of each other. Lightly oil the foil. Place the wrapped fish on the centre of the foil. Position the long sides of the foil together and fold over and over down towards the fish until it is wrapped loosely around the fish. Flatten and roll the ends of the foil towards the fish, making a good seal to keep in the butter once it begins to melt on the grill. (For foil-wrapping the fish, *see* the illustrations opposite.)

Barbecue Preheat the barbecue to medium-high or 'sizzle' temperature. Place the foil-wrapped fish on the grill. For the single large fish, cook on one side for 15–20 minutes. Turn and cook for a further 15 minutes on the other side. Test the fish for doneness using a temperature probe – first unroll the foil at the head end and pierce the flesh at the thickest point. When done, the probe will register 60C. Alternatively, have a peep inside the flesh, piercing it at its thickest point with a small sharp knife. Rewrap the fish and leave to sit on a warm tray for 10 minutes or so. If two 1.5kg fish, reduce the grill time to 12–15 minutes on the first and 12 minutes on the second side.

To serve Transfer the fish to a large serving platter still wrapped in the banana leaf. Surround with lime wedges and serve with Jamaican Rice and Peas (*see* page 160) and a crunchy leaf salad mixed with Guacamole (*see* page 190). We would also advise a bones bowl, warm lime-water finger bowls and paper napkins.

Salmon in Foil

Salmon becomes more than just salmon when cooked on a barbecue. Blistering have been known to cook individual salmon steaks for 100s of guests, but what a nightmare. Barbecuing whole sides of salmon wrapped in foil with whatever flavourings holds so many advantages. It produces a delicious succulent result every time, will never stick to the grill, the presentation is theatrical, the flavours are absorbed by the whole fish, there is more leeway in the grill timing and there's no turning, prodding or poking to be done.

If you're not buying a whole side of salmon, buy the thicker end of the fillet. Alternatively, use this method for individual fillet portions. Whatever you do, have your fish 'skinned and pinned' by your fishmonger – i.e. skin and bones removed.

To cook for 6 people You will need a 1.2kg piece of salmon fillet.

Wrapping Tear off 2 sheets of turkey foil, approximately 8 inches longer than your fillet. Do use good quality strong foil, as you really can't be doing with any tears. Brush the centre of the foil with oil where the salmon will sit. Before placing your fish on the oiled foil, strew and pour onto the oiled area any flavourings you are using. Be sure that you have turned up the edges of the foil sufficiently to prevent and liquids from flowing out. Place the fish on top of the flavourings, presentation side down (i.e. skinned side up). You are arranging the salmon and all ingredients upside-down, because the salmon will be inverted onto the serving dish once cooked. You will also find that having all the flavourings closer to the direct heat makes for great caramelisation.

With the salmon and flavourings in place, position the long sides of the foil together and fold over and over until it is wrapped loosely around the fish. Flatten and roll the ends of the foil towards the fish, making a good seal to keep in the juices and flavourings during the barbecuing process.

Barbecue This could not be easier. Heat the barbecue grill to medium-high. Place the parcel on the grill and cook – not turning at all – for approximately 12-15 minutes. Test for 'doneness' after 12 minutes. Unwrap an edge of the foil and have a peek, or use a temperature probe, which when inserted into the thickest part of the fillet will read 60C when the fish is cooked. Serve the fish straight away, or it will carry on cooking in its own steam.

To serve First select a serving plate or dish long enough to accommodate your fish and with a rim deep enough to hold any juices. Place the parcel on this plate and open the foil out. Tear the foil from the far side of the fillet so that you can flip the fish over off the foil and onto the plate. This is when you see the real value of cooking the fish upside-down, as the flavourings will have caramelised being so close to the direct heat.

Salmon Baked in Foil with Tangerine Juice, Tarragon and Crushed Pink Peppercorns

SERVES 6

• 2 hour marinade – not overnight

• One of the most popular Blistering salmon dishes.

1.2kg salmon fillet, skinned and de-boned

The flavourings
10 tangerines
1 tbsp pink peppercorns, crushed
4 shallots, finely chopped
2 tbsp chopped tarragon
sea salt and freshly ground black pepper

1 tbsp olive oil for brushing onto the foil

For the flavourings Juice 8 of the tangerines and pour the juice into a non-reactive saucepan. Add the pink peppercorns and shallots and bring to the boil. Simmer until the volume is reduced to a third. Leave to cool.

To wrap the fish Follow the instructions for barbecuing salmon in foil (*see* page 121).

In this case, for the flavourings, pour the tangerine mixture onto the oiled foil and scatter with the chopped tarragon. Season the salmon well on both sides with salt and pepper before placing on top of the flavourings. You can marinade the fish up to 2 hours before cooking.

If the salmon has been refrigerated, allow time for it to lose its chill before cooking on the barbecue.

Barbecue *See* instructions for cooking salmon in foil on page 121.

To serve To turn the salmon out of the foil, *see* instructions on page 121. Cut the remaining 2 tangerines into wedges and place in a bowl next to the fish. Serve with Vibrant Persian Rice Salad with Pine Nuts (*see* page 158) to soak up some of the delicious juices.

The mellow tang of the tangerine juice melds beautifully with the earthy taste of salmon.

Salmon Baked in Foil with Red Onion Confit, Tahini, Pinenuts and Lime

SERVES 6

• We picked this recipe up in Australia. Originally, it was served with mackerel, but we found that it was maybe a little too rich – with the less oily, but still substantial salmon, it proved to be something of a masterpiece.

1.2 kg salmon fillet, skinned and de-boned

For the flavourings
2 tbsp pine nuts
1 tbsp olive oil
4 tbsp Red Onion Confit (page 194)
Juice of 3 limes
Sea salt and freshly ground black pepper
2 tbsp runny tahini

1 tbsp olive oil
3 tbsp chopped coriander leaves

For the flavourings Toast the pine nuts on the hob in a dry skillet or frying pan, shaking the pan regularly to avoid over-colouring.

To wrap the fish Follow the instructions for wrapping salmon in foil, brushing the foil with the olive oil (*see* page 121). Spread the Red Onion Confit over the oiled area of the foil and scatter over the toasted pinenuts. Pour over the lime juice, distributing it evenly over the flavourings area. Season the fish on both sides with salt and pepper and place on top of the flavourings. Spread the Tahini over the skinned side of the fillet, which will be facing upwards at this point. You can wrap the fish up to 2 hours before cooking, but no longer as the lime juice will begin to 'cook' the flesh.

If the salmon has been refrigerated, allow time for it to lose its chill before cooking on the barbecue.

Barbecue *See* instructions for cooking salmon in foil on page 121.

To serve To turn the salmon out of the foil, *see* instructions on page 121. Scatter the cooked fish with the coriander. Serve with crusty bread and Vivid Green Salad with Beans (*see* page 171) and Puy Lentil Salad (*see* page 165).

A great twist on an Aussie recipe: a sensational yet terribly simple dish.

Chermoula-marinated Moroccan Salmon Baked in Foil served with Minted Yoghurt

SERVES 6

• 2 hour marinade

1.2kg salmon fillet, skinned and boned

For the Chermoula flavourings
1 tbsp cumin seeds
2 tsp coriander seeds
2 tsp ground ginger
1 tbsp mild paprika
3 cloves garlic, finely chopped
2-3 small red chillies, finely chopped (or to taste)
$1/2$ tsp freshly ground black pepper
zest of 2 lemons
1 level tsp fine sea salt
3 tbsp olive oil

3 tbsp chopped coriander leaves
3 tbsp chopped parsley leaves
3 spring onions, finely sliced on the diagonal
juice of 2 lemons

For the flavourings Toast the cumin and coriander seeds on the hob in a dry skillet or frying pan. Grind in a spice grinder or pestle and mortar. Mix these toasted ground spices with the ground ginger, paprika, garlic, chillies, pepper, lemon zest, salt and 2 tbsp of the olive oil, to produce a spreadable paste.

Spread this mixture evenly over the presentation side of the side of salmon.

To wrap the fish Follow the instructions for barbecuing salmon in foil, brushing the foil well with the remaining tbsp of oil (*see* page 121). In this case, the flavourings are already on the fish, so simply lie the fish spice-side down on the oiled foil. Season the other side with a little sea salt. You can wrap the fish up to 2 hours before cooking.

If the salmon has been refrigerated, allow time for it to lose its chill before cooking on the barbecue.

Barbecue *See* instructions for cooking salmon in foil on page 121.

To serve To turn the salmon out of the foil, *see* instructions on page 121. Scatter the cooked fish with the coriander, parsley and spring onions and sprinkle over the lemon juice. Serve with Cous Cous Salad (*see* page 161) and Crunchy Carrot Salad with Seeds (*see* page 170).

Moroccan-themed Blistering buffets go down a storm. This dish is always an integral part.

Barbecued Prawns

Shell on or shell off – that is the question. Either way, prawns are one of the most delicious and easiest natural food packages to grill on the barbecue.

We find that the best value large prawns are found in the freezer in oriental supermarkets. Make sure you buy raw – i.e. grey-blue in colour, not pink.

At home, we generally barbecue with the shell on – particularly if using the largest jumbo or king prawns or giant tiger varieties. The end result is more succulent, as the natural prawn juices bubble away on the grill where they are trapped under the shell. Some see the messiness of the peeling and eating process as a downside – we don't. We think the best food is worth grappling for. Undoubtedly, though, if you leave the shells on, the marinade flavours don't penetrate so easily through to the sweet prawn flesh – unless, that is, they are de-veined.

More often than not these days, prawns are farmed and pretty clean. If, however, you do find a dark vein running down the back of the prawn, it must be removed, as it contains the prawn's waste products. For shell-on prawns, place the prawn on its side on a chopping board and, using a strong serated-edged knife, saw through the outer shell and cut out the dirt trail. With shelled prawns, simply slice out the dirt trail with a sharp thin knife.

For a Blistering party, we find that peeled skewered prawns are ordered more often than not. It means less mess for the guests. We leave the head and tail on, de-vein and marinade. If the budget allows, we go for enormous jumbo prawns, which can reach the size of small lobsters. With these, we leave the shell on, as there is less fiddle at the table.

You need a really clean grill to barbecue prawns, as they do stick very easily, though you can avoid sticking completely by removing the grill and lying long flat metal skewers loaded with prawns across the barbecue trough.

Red Thai Prawns with Chilled Coconut, Lime & Coriander Sauce

SERVES 6

• 2 hour marinade

• Thai flavours go deliciously with prawns. Bought spice pastes can be great, but tend to maximise on chilli heat at the expense of the clean sour-sweet flavours that go so well with prawns. Try this homemade red curry paste, which keeps in the fridge for weeks. Serve with Chilled Coconut, Lime & Coriander Sauce.

700g raw peeled tiger prawns, de-veined
metal skewers

For the Red Curry Paste Marinade

1 tsp coriander seeds
1 tsp cumin seeds
4 sticks lemon grass, outer leaves discarded, finely chopped
1 inch piece of galangal, peeled and finely chopped
3 tsp dried shrimp
1 tbsp palm sugar + 1 tbsp water
6 large red chillies, deseeded and finely chopped (leave the seeds in if you like it hot)
4 cloves garlic, peeled and chopped
1 large thumb ginger, peeled and chopped
3 lime leaves, shredded
1 tbsp tomato purée
1 tbsp fish sauce

For grilling

fine sea salt
juice of one lime

Chilled Coconut, Lime & Coriander Sauce (see p184)

For the marinade Toast the coriander and cumin seeds in a dry skillet or frying pan. Grind in a spice grinder or pestle and mortar with the lemon grass, galangal and shrimp. Place a small pan on the heat and slowly melt the palm sugar in the water. Tip all the marinade ingredients into a blender and pulse to a smooth paste. Keep this paste in a tightly lidded jar. It will last for 2-3 weeks in the fridge.

To marinate the prawns Place the prawns in a bowl with 1 tbsp of the Red Curry Paste. Distribute the marinade evenly over the surface of the prawns. Thread onto stainless steel skewers, skewering firstly through the thick head-end and then through the tail of each prawn. Lining up the prawns in this way makes for even cooking on the barbecue. Cover and refrigerate. Marinade for at least 2 hours. Overnight is unnecessary, but fine. Before barbecuing, give the prawns enough time out of the fridge to lose their chill. Season with salt to taste.

Barbecue Preheat the grill to medium-high or 'sizzle' temperature. Clean and lightly oil the rack. Grill the prawn skewers for 2-3 minutes on each side until the prawns are firm, but not charred and shrinking. Be very careful, as prawns are incredibly devalued by over-cooking. They will continue to cook for a couple of minutes after you remove them from the barbecue.

To serve Using a fork, push the prawns off the skewers, a couple at a time so as not to damage them, onto a serving plate. Sprinkle with the fresh lime juice and more seasoning if required. Serve with the Coconut, Lime & Coriander Sauce, Egg Noodle Salad (*see* page 162) and Thai Green Papaya Salad (*see* page 166).

Tips This recipe is sublime with small lobster tails, which you can buy frozen with head and claws removed. Split the tails lengthways through the belly, leaving the shell intact so that the tails will retain their shape on the grill. Make sure that the marinade penetrates into the split to reach the flesh within. You don't need skewers. Grill as above, for 8-10 minutes, turning regularly.

The clean sour-sweet-salty flavours of Thailand are perfect for prawns.

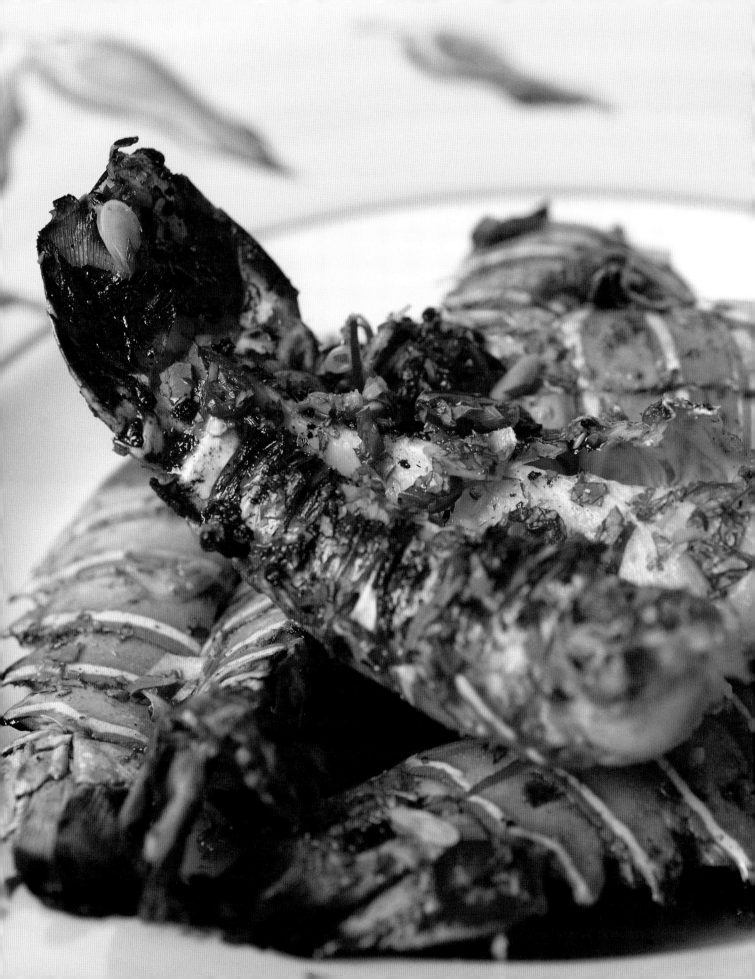

Marinated Squid and Chips with Fresh Rocket and Red and Green Salsas

SERVES 6

- 2 hour to overnight marinade

- The red and green salsas look great on the plate. Best chips for the job in our opinion are shoestring.

1kg cleaned squid

For the marinade
4 cloves garlic, finely chopped
$1/2$ medium-sized red onion, finely sliced
2 large red chillies, finely diced (include the seeds for extra heat)
1 bunch flat parsley, finely chopped
zest of one lemon
2 tbsp olive oil
$1/2$ tsp freshly ground black pepper

For grilling
fine sea salt
juice of one lemon

To serve
sea salt
shoestring fries
rocket leaves
juice of $1/2$ lemon
2 tbsp olive oil
Fresh Tomato Salsa (*see* page 193)
Roughly Chopped Fresh Green Salsa (*see* page 192)

To prepare the squid Slice down one side of the squid tube, so that it opens out flat on a chopping board. If the fishmonger hasn't done so already, discard the transparent plastic-like quill and the guts and wash the squid under cold running water. Pat dry with paper towel. Using a sharp cook's knife, score the inner, softer side of the opened tube with a neat diamond pattern. Score no further than halfway through the flesh. Cut the scored tube in half, making two triangular pieces. If you want to use the tentacles, cut the head below the eyes and squeeze out the beak. Discard the beak and head. The ring that holds the tentacles together can be quite thick, so cut the tentacles into bundles so that the ring piece will cook at the same rate as the rest of the squid.

To marinate the squid Combine the marinade ingredients in a bowl. Toss with the squid. Transfer to a strong plastic bag, or cover with clingfilm and refrigerate. Leave to marinate for at least 2 hours, or preferably overnight.

Before barbecuing Give the squid enough time out of the fridge to lose its chill. Season with sea salt. Have your fries or chips ready for the fryer or the oven.

Squid must be cooked quickly: If cooked slowly, it becomes tough and rubbery.

Barbecue Preheat the grill to high or 'searing' temperature. Squid is a notorious sticker, so thoroughly clean and lightly oil the rack. Grill times depend on the thickness of the squid tubes and tentacle ring. On average, the tentacles take a total of 5-7 minutes and

A terrific summery Bistro-style dish.

the scored tube pieces 4-5 minutes to grill, so place the tentacles on the barbecue first and grill for 1-2 minutes before adding the scored tube pieces. Place the squid tube pieces, scored side down on the barbecue and grill for 2-3 minutes on the scored side. Turn and grill for a further 2 minutes. Take all the squid off the grill and squeeze over the lemon juice, which helps to tenderise the squid. Serve straight away.

To serve Dress the rocket to taste with lemon juice, olive oil and seasoning. Plate the squid with a handful of fries, the dressed leaves and a spoonful of each of the salsas.

Seared Keralan Tuna Steaks with Mild Indian Spices, Minted Mustard Seed & Cucumber Raita and Salty Onion, Chilli & Lemon Relish SERVES 6

• 2 hour marinade

• Tuna is a game fish, and being robust and meaty, can take and indeed benefits from stronger flavours. Like all fish, it suffers greatly from overcooking, becoming dried out and flavourless, so take great care on the grill. Once again, practice makes perfect.

• You can buy tamarind in different forms, but we find that the rough dried pulp, still containing the stones makes for the best flavour.... But use the ready-made tamarind paste if you prefer.

• If you can get to an Asian supermarket, do try to get your hands on mango powder. It has a great flavour, adding texture and sweetness to marinades. It's a favourite on the Blistering Top Shelf.

6 x 175g tuna steaks, ideally cut 3cm thick

For the marinade
3 tsp tamarind pulp
3 tsp cumin seeds
2 tsp coriander seeds
1 tsp fenugreek seeds
2 large mild green chillies, finely sliced, or to taste
1 tsp cayenne pepper
2 tsp garlic powder or 1 tsp garlic granules
2 tsp mango powder (optional)

To grill and serve
vegetable oil for brushing
fine sea salt and freshly ground black pepper
2 limes

For the marinade Place the tamarind in a teacup or small bowl with 4 teaspoons of boiling water. Leave to soften for 20-25 minutes, mashing occasionally with the back of the spoon to extract all the flavour.

Push through a sieve with the back of a spoon into a bowl. Toast the cumin, coriander and fenugreek seeds in a dry skillet or frying pan. Grind in a spice grinder or pestle and mortar. Mix with the prepared tamarind and all the other marinade ingredients.

To marinate the fish Spread the paste equally over both sides of all six tuna steaks. Cover and refrigerate for at least 2 hours or overnight won't do any harm.

Before barbecuing Give the tuna steaks enough time out of the fridge to lose their chill. Brush both sides of each steak lightly with vegetable oil and season well with salt and pepper.

Barbecue Preheat the barbecue grill to high or 'searing' temperature. Clean and lightly oil the rack. The following timings are for a 3cm thick steak cooked pink. If thinner, adjust the grill time accordingly. Place the steaks on the grill and cook for 2 minutes. Do not attempt to move the fish until the flesh begins to mark and so release itself from, or if you like, burn itself off the grill bars. Use a fish slice to turn the steaks. Grill for a further 2 minutes on the flip side, or until well marked.

To serve Remove the crusted seared tuna steaks to a serving plate and surround with lime wedges. Serve with Minted Mustard Seed & Cucumber Raita (*see* page 194) and Salty Onion, Chilli & Lemon Relish (*see* page 195).

Tuna is at its best just seared – marked with the grill bars on either side, but rosy in the middle.

Sugar and Spice Swordfish
with Pineapple, Pepper & Chilli Salsa

SERVES 6

• 2 hour marinade or overnight

• Stay with your fish as you barbecue it. Perfectly cooked swordfish is succulent heaven: overcooked, it is cardboard hell.

6 x 175g swordfish steaks, cut approximately 2cm thick

For the marinade
2 tsp cumin seeds
1 tsp coriander seeds
2 tsp cayenne pepper
$1/2$ tsp ground allspice
1 thumb fresh ginger, peeled and finely chopped
2 tsp chopped oregano

To grill and serve
vegetable oil for brushing
fine sea salt and freshly ground black pepper
Pineapple, Pepper and Chilli Salsa (see page 190)

To marinate the fish Toast the cumin and coriander seeds in a dry skillet or frying pan. Grind in a spice grinder or pestle and mortar. Tip into a roomy bowl and mix with the other marinade ingredients. Place the swordfish steaks in the bowl and using disposable gloves, rub them evenly on both sides with the marinade. Cover and leave to marinate for at least two hours.

Before barbecuing Give the swordfish steaks enough time out of the fridge to lose their chill. Brush both sides of each steak lightly with vegetable oil and season well with salt and pepper.

Barbecue Preheat the barbecue grill to medium–high or 'sizzle' temperature. Clean and lightly oil the rack. Place the steaks on the grill and cook for 2–3 minutes (for a 2cm thick steak). Do not attempt to move the fish until the flesh begins to mark and so release itself from, or if you like, burn itself off the grill bars. Use a fish slice to turn the steaks. Grill for a further 2–3 minutes on the flip side, or until well marked and just cooked through. Naturally, grill time will vary depending on the thickness of the steaks.

To serve Remove the crusted swordfish to a serving plat. Serve with the Pineapple, Pepper & Chilli Salsa and Persian Rice Salad (see page 158).

Tips We can't stress enough how important it is not to overcook swordfish. It is better to take the fish off slightly undercooked and to trap the heat under foil allowing the fish to steam to complete the cooking process, rather than drying it out on the grill.

The warmth of spices and the sweet tang of fruit sit very well together on game fish.

Spiced Middle Eastern Monkfish and Scallop Skewers with Mint & Pomegranate Molasses Dipping Sauce

SERVES 6 AS A STARTER

- 2 hour marinade, or overnight is fine

- This simple, but fairly rich fish skewer is great as a starter, main course or as a tapas plate. Simply double the ingredients if serving as a main course.
- Bamboo skewers look great, but you must soak them in water for at least 30 minutes before using them.

6 king-size scallops, trimmed of any grey sinews
500g monkfish tail, cut into 12 approximately 3 cm chunks
6 x 6 inch metal or soaked bamboo skewers

For the marinade
2 tsp cumin seeds
1 tsp sumac powder
1/2 tsp freshly ground pepper
2 tbsp olive oil

To grill and serve
olive oil
fine sea salt
Pomegranate Molasses & Mint Dipping Sauce
  (see page 195)
1 lime, cut into 6 wedges

To marinate and thread the skewers
Toast the cumin seeds in a dry skillet or frying pan. Grind in a spice grinder or pestle and mortar. Mix in a bowl with the other marinade ingredients. Roll the scallops and monkfish chunks in the marinade. Skewer one piece of monkfish through the middle, then a scallop, piercing first the orange coral (if you have left it on) and then through the heart of the white muscle and then through another piece of monkfish. Repeat with the remaining 5 skewers, using up all the fish and shellfish. Cover tightly with clingfilm and refrigerate for at least 2 hours. Overnight is fine but unnecessary.

Before barbecuing Give the skewers enough time out of the fridge to lose their chill. Brush all sides lightly with olive oil and season well with salt. Gently warm up the Pomegranate Molasses & Mint Dipping Sauce.

Barbecue Preheat the barbecue to high, or 'scaring' temperature. If you have height control, place your rack as close to the hot coals as you can. Clean and lightly oil the rack. Place the skewers on the grill and cook for 2 minutes on each of two sides, or until just cooked. Scallops and monkfish will continue to cook for a couple of minutes after being removed from the grill.

To serve Serve the skewers on warm plates with a drizzle of the warmed pomegranate sauce and a wedge of lime.

This is a great way to kick off a barbecue fish extravaganza.

Hot Cured and Gun-Powder-Tea-Smoked Salmon with Sweet Mustard & Dill Sauce

SERVES 6

• Overnight cure

• Smoking fresh fish is addictive. The results are deliciously moist and full of flavour. In this recipe, there are two stages to the flavouring and cooking; first the curing and then the smoking. You can use either a wood-fired oven, or a lidded barbecue.

• For a great smoky flavour, here we suggest sprinkling soaked Gunpowder Tea onto your embers. This tea can be bought in delis and particularly in Middle Eastern supermarkets where it is used in fresh mint tea. You might also like to try soaking coarse herbs, such as rosemary or thyme. Soaked hickory wood chips also add a great layer of flavour. You can buy hickory chips in any well-stocked DIY store in the summer months.

• This is such a versatile technique. At Blistering we experiment endlessly with ingredients. *See* other suggestions in Tips at the end of this recipe.

1.2kg salmon fillet in one piece, skinned and pinned by your fishmonger

To cure
90g sea salt
225g white sugar
5 tbsp chopped dill
zest of 1 large lemon

To smoke
150g gunpowder tea, green tea or Lapsang Souchong

To serve
Sweet Mustard & Dill Sauce (*see* page 182)

To cure the salmon Mix the cure ingredients together. Pull out a length of clingfilm 15cm longer than your piece of salmon. (Do not cut the clingfilm, as you will be folding it back over the top of the fish to enclose the cure). Sprinkle half of the cure over the unrolled clingfilm covering an area the size of the salmon fillet. Place the fillet onto the cure and sprinkle the other half evenly over the top of the fish. Roll the clingfilm back over to envelope the fish. Fold up the ends and the sides of the clingfilm to wrap the salmon well. Transfer to a tray at least 2cm deep to ensure that juices do not dribble over your fridge during the curing process. Place a weighted flat tray on top of the fish. For the weight use a tray loaded with a few one-litre packs of fruit juice, a 6-pack of lager or equivalent. Leave to cure in the fridge overnight or for approximately 12 hours.

To prepare to smoke the salmon While you are lighting your fire, soak the gunpowder tea in water for at least 30 minutes. Wash the salmon thoroughly to get rid of any salt and sugar cure mixture and pat dry with kitchen paper. Cut the salmon side into 6 equal portions and place on a metal tray lined with baking parchment, taking care that the parchment does not hang over the edges of the tray where it could catch fire.

Barbecue If using the wood-fired oven, make a small fire of small hardwood logs using newspaper for kindling (*see* page 24). If using the barbecue, make a similar fire in one side of the barbecue pit. When the logs have burnt down to hot embers, you are ready to start smoking. Sprinkle the soaked tea leaves onto the burning embers. Place the tray either on the base of the wood-fired oven and close the door, or on the cooler side of the barbecue grill and put the lid on. Either way, a little air will get in to keep the fire smouldering. The salmon should be smoked through with a lovely tan smoky colour within 7–10 minutes. Cooking time will vary according to the heat of your oven and the thickness of the fillet.

To serve Serve with hot new potatoes, Sweet Mustard & Dill Sauce (*see* page 182) and a crispy green salad. This is also sensational with Hollandaise Sauce (*see* page 180).

Tips For an Asian angle, try adding dried chilli flakes, Szechwan peppercorns and chopped fresh ginger to the cure mix. Add soaked star anise and coriander seeds to the embers. For Moroccan flavours in the cure, use coriander root, saffron, sumac and dried ground ginger. Add soaked cinnamon bark and cloves to the embers.

VEGETABLE DISHES

Mediterranean Vegetable Skewers with Peppers, Red Onions and Courgettes drizzled with Rocket Pesto

MAKES 6 STARTERS / SIDE DISHES

• No marinade necessary, but can be prepared the day before.

• On Blistering buffets, there is always at least one barbecued vegetable dish and this simple skewer makes a popular warm salad, not only with vegetarians, but also with meat eaters. We also use it as tapas, as part of a mezze plate, as a starter with fresh Buffalo Mozzarella and as the main ingredient of a sensational sandwich (*see* page 63).

For the skewers
2 large red peppers
1 large yellow pepper
2 medium red onions
450g courgettes (the smaller they are, the firmer they are)
2 tbsp olive oil
fine sea salt and freshly ground black pepper
6 x 30cm metal skewers, or equivalent

To serve
Rocket Pesto (*see* page 182)

To prepare the vegetables Cut the peppers in half through the stem and remove the stem, any seeds and white pith. Cut each half into three lengthways, and each of the resulting pieces into two, so that each pepper is cut into twelve pieces. Peel the red onions, but do not remove the root, as this will hold the cut onion wedges together. Cut the two onions straight down through the root and then each half into three wedges, giving a total of 12. Trim off each end of the courgettes and slice into 2cm lengths.

To prepare the skewers Place the prepared vegetables in a bowl and toss with the olive oil. Season well with salt and pepper. Thread the vegetables, mixed up, onto the metal skewers. Skewer the courgettes through the skin, not through the soft seedy middle. Either use straight away or refrigerate for the next day.

If the skewers have been refrigerated, allow time for them to lose their chill before cooking on the barbecue.

Barbecue Preheat the grill to medium-high or 'sizzle' temperature. Clean and lightly oil the rack. Place the skewers on the grill and cook for 12-15 minutes, turning every 2-3 minutes, or until the vegetables are gently charred around the edges. You may have to move the skewers to a medium heat at some point to prevent over-charring before the red onions soften. When the onions have softened, the rest will be cooked. If the vegetables aren't to be served immediately, transfer them to a lidded terracotta or oven-proof dish to keep their heat and to prevent drying out.

To serve Push the vegetables off the skewers with a fork onto serving plates and drizzle the the Rocket Pesto over them.

Warm Spice-Crusted Butternut Squash with Goat's Cheese, Spring Onions, Toasted Pumpkin Seeds and Coriander & Ginger Pesto   MAKES 6 MAIN COURSES

- 2 hour to overnight marinade

- A stunning autumnal centrepiece dish. Once grilled, the marinade takes the form of a delicious crust. Use a soft, ripe goat's cheese that will melt easily. These days, you can get your hands on butternut squash all year round.
- You'll need an ovenproof dish and hinged sandwich racks.

900g butternut squash

For the Spice Crust marinade
1 tbsp cumin seeds
$^1/_2$ tbsp coriander seeds
$^1/_4$ tsp ground allspice
3 tsp sumac powder
1 tbsp mild paprika

12 spring onions, washed and trimmed
3 tbsp olive oil
fine sea salt and freshly ground black pepper
350g ripe soft goat's cheese
1$^1/_2$ tbsp dried pumpkin seeds
Coriander & Ginger Pesto (*see* page 187)

To prepare the squash Top, tail and, using a potato peeler, peel the squash. Using a heavy kitchen knife, cut each squash in half lengthways. Scoop out the seeds. Place each half flat-side down, and, beginning at the solid end, cut into 1$^1/_2$ cm thick semi-circular pieces. When you reach the bulbous end where the seeds were, the flesh is thinner and softer, so increase the thickness of the slices to 2cm. This way, all the pieces of squash will cook at the same pace. Blanch the squash in a pan of boiling salted water for 4-5 minutes, or until *al dente*. Take care not to overcook. Drain in a colander and refresh under cold running water to stop the cooking process. Drain well.

For the marinade Heat a dry frying pan or skillet. Add the cumin and coriander seeds and toast until aromatic, shaking from time to time to prevent burning. Transfer to the spice grinder or pestle and mortar and blitz or grind to a powder. Mix with the other marinade ingredients.

In a large bowl, toss the pumpkin and the whole spring onions with the olive oil. Sprinkle over the marinade, distributing it as evenly as possible. Season well with salt and pepper. Slice the goat's cheese into pieces of one to two bites in size. Toast the pumpkin seeds in a dry skillet or frying pan for a couple of minutes, or until picking up a little colour.

Barbecue Preheat the hinged sandwich racks or grill to medium-high or 'sizzle' temperature. Clean and lightly oil the rack. Place the squash in hinged sandwich racks on the grill and cook on the first side for 4-5 minutes until nicely coloured. Turn the rack over, open it up and pop in the spring onions on the charred side of the squash. Close it again and cook the other side of the squash for a further 4 minutes, or until cooked through and nicely coloured. Turn the rack again to lightly char the spring onions for 1 minute. Transfer the squash and onions to a terracotta or ovenproof dish and top first with the goats cheese and then with the spring onions. Scatter with toasted pumpkin seeds and cover with foil or a lid. Place the terracotta on the barbecue to heat through until the cheese begins to melt – at least 7 minutes.

To serve Let your guests help themselves. Serve with a dressed leaf salad, some toasted bread and a bowl of Coriander & Ginger Pesto.

Tips Coriander and Ginger Pesto is quite a stiff sauce, so if you want to drizzle it, let it down slowly with some olive oil.

Aloo Gobi and Paneer Skewers (potato, cauliflower and Indian cheese) with Pickle Tray

MAKES 6 STARTERS / SIDE DISHES

- 3 hour to overnight marinade

- Cauliflower takes on a different identity when seasoned and charred. In India, the florets are browned in oil in a korai, or Indian cast iron wok. Here we do a similar thing on the barbecue. The Indian cheese paneer has a fantastic texture and has proved to be a great success on the barbecue.
- The cut flesh of the potato absorbs the flavours of the spice mix infinitely more effectively than the skin, so this recipe uses large new potatoes, which have to be cut down to size to thread onto the skewer. If you would prefer to use small potatoes, you'd have to peel them to get the same effect.

For the marinade
1 tsp cumin seeds
2 tsp coriander seeds
1 tsp fennel seeds
1 tsp cayenne pepper
2 tsp turmeric
1 tsp ground ginger
3 tsp garam masala
1/2 tsp freshly ground black pepper
1/2 tsp fine sea salt

For the skewers
1kg large new potatoes, scrubbed
1/2 medium cauliflower
3 tbsp vegetable oil
500g paneer cheese, 2.5 cm dice
4 x 30cm metal skewers, or bamboo skewer equivalent, soaked in water for 1/2 hour

To serve
1 tsp toasted cumin seeds
fresh red chillies, deseeded and finely diced
chopped fresh coriander, to taste
mango chutney
Minted Mustard Seed & Cucumber Raita (see page 194)
Salty Onion, Chilli & Lemon Relish (see page 195)

For the spice mix Toast the cumin, coriander and fennel seeds in a dry skillet or frying pan. Grind in a spice grinder or pestle and mortar. Mix in a small bowl or cup with the remaining marinade ingredients.

To prepare the skewers Cook the whole potatoes in a large pan of boiling salted water for 12-15 minutes, or until almost cooked through. Strain through a colander and return them to the pan. Leave under a running cold tap for 1 minute to arrest the cooking process. Drain again. Cut the potatoes into 3cm square-ish chunks. Cut the cauliflower into florets a similar size to the potato chunks. Blanch the florets in boiling salted water for 2 minutes. Drain and plunge into iced water to arrest the cooking process. Drain again. Place the cooked potato chunks, cauliflower florets and paneer in a bowl and toss with the vegetable oil. Sprinkle over the marinade spice mix and toss, distributing the flavours evenly.

Our take on an Indian restaurant classic.

Thread the potatoes, cauliflower and paneer cheese, mixed up, onto the skewers. Cover and refrigerate overnight or for at least 3 hours.

Barbecue Preheat the grill to medium-high or 'sizzle' temperature. Clean and lightly oil the rack. Place the skewers on the grill and cook for 3-4 minutes on each of four sides, or until the vegetables and cheese are gently charred around the edges.

To serve Serve on or off the skewers, sprinkled with whole toasted cumin seeds, chopped chilli and chopped fresh coriander and accompanied by a pickle tray of mango chutney, Minted Mustard Seed & Cucumber Raita (*see* page 194) and Salty Onion, Chilli & Lemon Relish (*see* page 195).

Plantain and Onion Skewers with Fresh Red Chilli

MAKES 6 SIDE DISHES

- You may have passed Asian food shops and wondered what those large ripe plantains taste like. They look like bananas, but taste totally different. This recipe presents a very easy way for you to try them out. Next time you see them, pick a few up, try out the following and enjoy it on its own, or as a side dish that goes brilliantly with any Asian or Caribbean barbecue dish. Plantains come in different stages of ripeness – green, yellow and black. For this recipe, they need to still have some yellow colour, but be moving towards total blackness.
- For true authenticity, you should use the lantern-shaped scotch bonnet chillies, but they may be too much of a shock to the system. In the early days, we used to use these alarmingly hot chillies as decoration on Bites trays, but found that they were ruining too many people's evenings.

2 large ripe plantains (yellow and black, but mostly black)
6 large spring onions
2 tbsp palm oil or vegetable oil
2 red scotch bonnet or 4 mild red chillies, deseeded and finely chopped or diced
fine sea salt and freshly ground black pepper
6 x 15cm bamboo skewers, soaked in water for 1/2 hour
chopped fresh coriander, to taste

To prepare the skewers Peel the plantains, as you would a banana. Cut into 4cm lengths and then in half through the middle, exposing the middle of the plantain. Chop the spring onion into 2.5cm lengths, reserving the green tops to chop finely and sprinkle over the finished dish. Toss the plantain and onion in a bowl with the oil and chopped chilli. Season with salt and pepper to taste. Thread the plantain and spring onion onto the bamboo skewers, starting and finishing each skewer with plantain. Use within 3 hours to avoid discolouring.

Barbecue Preheat the grill to medium. You need to cook the plantains fairly slowly to allow time for the natural sugars to caramelise. Clean and lightly oil the rack. Place the skewers on the grill and cook for 8-10 minutes, turning every 2-3 minutes, or until plantains and onions are cooked through and gently charred around the edges.

To serve Finely chop the reserved spring onion tops. Pile the skewers on a serving plate and sprinkle with the onion tops and chopped fresh coriander. Serve with Jerked Rack of Ribs (seee page 108), Jamaican Rice and Peas (*see* page 160), Sour Cream & Chives (*see* page 190) and a fiery pepper sauce if you fancy.

Roasted Field Mushrooms Topped with Thyme, Cambazola, Chives and plenty of Salt and Pepper

MAKES 6 MAIN COURSES

- This is a great dish for vegetarians. Not being veggies ourselves, we enjoy them with Butterflied Leg of Lamb, new potatoes, leaf salad and a glass of red wine.
- Remember when you are buying your mushrooms, that they shrink by a third when cooked. Never wash mushrooms – and particularly field mushrooms; just wipe them: they absorb water like sponges.
- Cambazola is a mass-produced cheese, but is great for this recipe. You could use Gorgonzola, but we find that the former is not quite so strong and gives a lovely creamy finish to the dish.
- This is one dish where hinged sandwich racks really help to prevent the olive oil and cheese from spilling onto the coals. It also means that all the mushrooms are put onto the grill at the same time, so will all be finished together.

12 large flat field mushrooms (700g approximately)
1 tbsp finely chopped fresh thyme
sea salt and freshly ground black pepper
6 tbsp olive oil, approximately
175g Cambazola or any soft blue cheese
chives, snipped into 1cm lengths, to taste

To prepare the mushrooms Brush or wipe your mushrooms clean of any bits of dirt. Place them gill-side-up on metal trays, or if you have removable handled grill racks, straight onto these. Sprinkle with the thyme and season well with salt and pepper. Drizzle each mushroom with olive oil. Transfer the mushrooms, gill-side-up from the trays to the barbecue, or place the removable grill racks over the coals. Slice the Cambazola thinly and, for ease of handling, lay the slices on greaseproof paper.

Barbecue Preheat the grill to medium-high or 'sizzle' temperature. Clean and lightly oil the rack. Grill the mushrooms, gill-side-up for approximately 5 minutes. You will not be turning them over, as you would lose all the juices. When the skin is nicely charred, using a fish slice, remove the mushrooms from the grill straight back onto the metal trays. Top with slices of Cambazola and sprinkle with the chives. Return the whole trays of topped mushrooms to the barbecue grill and leave there for a further 5 minutes, or until the cheese has warmed through and starts to melt.

To serve Serve hot with bread to soak up the juices.

Grilled Fennel with Beef Tomatoes, Fresh Mozzarella and Salmariglio

MAKES A SALAD FOR 6

- This dish shouts *al fresco* very loudly. A stunning sunny summertime accompaniment to any grilled fish dish. Fennel must be cooked relatively slowly and is simply fantastic cooked in the wood-fired oven, but the barbecue also produces a flavour all of its own.
- Salmariglio is a pungent fresh herb sauce from Italy – tantalising to the taste buds. It should be drizzled sparingly over this dish.

2 large, or 3 medium-sized heads of fennel
3 tbsp olive oil
fine sea salt and freshly ground black pepper
500g beef tomatoes, or equivalent tasty tomatoes
250g Buffalo Mozzarella
1 tbsp balsamic vinegar

1¹/₂ tbsp Salmariglio (*see* page 182)
extra virgin olive oil (optional)

Trim any stems off the top of the fennel bulb, retaining any of the feathery leaves to scatter over the finished salad. Discard any bruised leathery outer layers. You want to retain the root and hard heart of the fennel to hold your finished wedges together, so if the root end has discoloured, clean it up by taking off the thinnest of slices. Cut the fennel heads in half and then slice each half into 3-4 mm thick wedges or 'fans', each time cutting through the root and heart to keep the fan in one piece. Place the fennel in a bowl, drizzle over the olive oil and season well with salt and pepper.

Barbecue Preheat the grill to medium or 'cook' temperature. Clean and lightly oil the rack. Place the fennel on the grill and cook slowly for up to 20 minutes, or until softened. If the fennel is picking up too much colour, move it to a cooler area of the grill, or place on a piece of foil on the grill. If fennel is not cooked for long enough, it will be stringy and chewy.

To serve Leave the fennel to cool on the side. Do not refrigerate, as this salad is best served at room temperature. Slice the beef tomatoes and Mozzarella into rounds, or half moons, as you prefer. Season your tomatoes with salt and pepper and drizzle with balsamic vinegar and olive oil if desired. Arrange the tomatoes, fennel and Mozzarella on a serving plate and drizzle sparingly with Salmariglio. Scatter over fennel leaves, if you have any.

A stunning summer salad, rich with the flavours of the Mediterranean.

Turkish Aubergines with Creamy Garlic Yoghurt

MAKES 6 MAIN COURSES

- The terrific climate of the Fertile Crescent produces piles of plump ripe ingredients allowing Turkish cooks to rustle up a fantastic array of salads and vegetable dishes. Even the most obscure back-street restaurant will have a great selection for you to choose from. And if you're by the sea, you can select your own freshly caught fish to be grilled and served with the salads of your choice. *Al fresco* paradise.
- Here's our recipe for the universally popular aubergine salad. The barbecued aubergines are thrown into a tomato 'salsita' – a half raw and half cooked sauce – and layered with cool garlic yoghurt.

1 kg (about 3) aubergines
2 tbsp olive oil (approximately), for brushing
sea salt and freshly ground black pepper

For the Salsita
1 red onion
3 tbsp olive oil
2 cloves garlic, finely chopped
1 x 400g top quality tin chopped plum tomatoes plus 1/2 tin water
1 tbsp chopped marjoram
2 large beef tomatoes, chopped into 2cm chunks
sea salt and freshly ground black pepper

For the Garlic Yoghurt
6 tbsp thick creamy natural yoghurt
1 clove garlic, finely chopped
sea salt and freshly ground black pepper

1 tbsp extra virgin olive oil (optional)
3 tbsp toasted pinenuts

To prepare the aubergine Wash and thinly peel the aubergines using a potato peeler. Slice into rings approximately 11/2cm thick. Brush lightly with olive oil on both sides. Season with salt and pepper. Set aside ready for the barbecue.

To make the Salsita Peel the red onion and cut in half straight down through the root. Slice the onion very thinly into half-rounds. Heat up the olive oil in a non-reactive pan. Add the sliced red onion and the 2 cloves of garlic. Sweat for a couple of minutes and add the tin of tomatoes and water. Cook on a medium heat for 15-20 minutes or until the tomatoes are well broken down and 'cooked out'. Take off the heat and add the chopped marjoram. Leave to cool before mixing in the chopped beef tomato. Season to taste with salt and pepper.

To prepare the Garlic Yoghurt Mix the yoghurt with the garlic. Season with salt and pepper to taste. Cover tightly with clingfilm and refrigerate.

Barbecue Preheat the hinged sandwich racks to medium-high, or 'sizzle' temperature. Clean and lightly oil the rack. Place the aubergines into the racks and grill on both sides for a total of 6-7 minutes, turning from time to time. The flesh must be browned before you attempt to move them from the rack: try too early and they will stick. When browned and softened, using a fish slice, remove the aubergines from the rack and drop them directly into the salsita. Mix up the aubergine salad and allow to cool.

To assemble the salad Spoon half of the aubergine tomato salad into the base of a flat-bottomed dish. Spread the garlic yoghurt over the top. Carefully spoon the second layer of aubergine and tomato salad over the yoghurt, so that no yoghurt can be seen. Drizzle over the tablespoon of extra virgin olive oil and sprinkle with the toasted pinenuts. Serve either cold, or at room temperature.

To serve Serve Turkish-style with any grilled fish and crusty bread for wiping up the juices.

Chargrilled Bok Choi and Red Peppers marinated in Thai Lime, Chilli & Coriander Syrup

MAKES A SALAD FOR 6

- This is a stunning dish of jewel-like colours. Tangy and mellow at the same time, it makes a great accompaniment to any oriental main course.
- You can make a more substantial dish for vegetarians, by adding barbecued haloumi (*see* Grilled Haloumi and Mediterranean Vegetable Sandwich on page 63).

700g bok choi (baby if available)
3 red peppers
1 tbsp vegetable oil
fine sea salt and freshly ground black pepper

To serve
4 tbsp Thai Lime, Chilli & Coriander Syrup
  (*see* page 186)

To prepare the vegetables If your bok choi are large, cut them in two through the root. Blanch the bok choi in a large pan of boiling salted water for 2 minutes. Drain through a colander, and refresh immediately with cold running water to arrest the cooking process. Drain well and dry thoroughly by laying on a clean tea towel or kitchen paper. Cut the peppers in half through the stem and remove the stem and seeds. Cut each half into three lengthways and slice out the white pith. Place red pepper pieces in a bowl and toss with the oil. Season to taste.

Barbecue Preheat the grill to medium-high, or 'sizzl'e temperature. Clean and lightly oil the rack. Place the peppers on the grill and grill for 4-5 minutes each side, or until softened. Towards the end of the pepper grilling process, grill the bok choi. Before placing the bok choi on the grill, fold the thin green leaves over onto the white fleshy parts. Place the bok choi onto the grill, with the more delicate green-side-up and grill for around 4-5 minutes on this side. Turn and dry out the green side for just 1-2 minutes.

To serve Remove all the hot vegetables to a serving dish. While still hot, drizzle with the Thai Lime, Chilli & Coriander Syrup. Allow to cool down and serve at room temperature.

Tips Serve with Thai Poussin (*see* page 76) and steamed Jasmine Rice. Alternatively, make skewers using the Bites recipe for Green Thai Chicken (*see* page 42) and serve with Coconut Curry Dipping Sauce (*see* page 186).

Autumnal Wood-roast Roots and Vegetables with Marjoram

MAKES 6 LARGE SIDE DISHES

- We love these vegetables at Blistering. So do our clients. We always roast extra as they prove very popular every time. The wood-fired oven produces the richest sweetest caramelisation of the roots. These vegetables make a fantastic accompaniment to any main course dish that's up there in the flavour league.
- Any leftovers add unbeatable flavour to a winter soup.

250g baby beetroots
500g parsnips, peeled
500g carrots, peeled
500g leeks, washed
250g fennel, washed
250g red onions
6 tbsp olive oil
fine sea salt and freshly ground black pepper
1 tbsp chopped marjoram

To prepare the vegetables Boil the baby beetroots in their skins for around 45 minutes, or until *al dente*. Top and tail the parsnips, cut into quarters lengthways and slice out the woody core. Top and tail the carrots and cut into chunky batons measuring approximately 1.5cm wide and 8cm long. Cut the leeks on the angle into 2cm wide slices and place into a bowl of water to wash. Drain through a colander. Cut the fennel heads as described in the method of the fennel recipe on page 146.

Peel the red onions, but do not remove the root, as this will hold the cut onion wedges together. Cut the onions straight down through the root and then each half into three or four wedges. Each vegetable will have to be roasted separately, as they cook at different rates, so have two trays on the go at any one time. You will need a non-reactive tray for roasting the onions. Drizzle all the vegetables with olive oil and season well with salt and pepper.

To roast in a wood-fired oven Start the roasting process for each vegetable in the hottest part of the oven i.e. on the trivet. Once the first tray begins to take some colour, move it to the base of the oven and place the next vegetable on the trivet. Carry on rotating in this way until all the vegetables are cooked through. Using this method, you won't end up with vegetables burnt on the outside and hard in the middle. Keep the roasted vegetables warm.

To serve Mix the warm vegetables together in a bowl. Sprinkle with the fresh chopped marjoram.

Tips These vegetables are also delicious cooked on the barbecue, but you will have to blanch all the roots until *al dente* before grilling. Toss with a little oil and season to taste before grilling.

Wood-roasting produces the richest, sweetest caramelisation of roast vegetables.

Mediterranean Wood-roast or Barbecued Vegetables with Pinenuts, Parmesan Shavings and Basil   MAKES 6 MAIN COURSES

• This dish is without doubt at its most spectacular out of the wood-fired oven. The speed with which this oven roasts leaves the vegetables succulent with a fantastic charred smoky flavour.
The barbecue, however, produces a delicious second-best.

1 large aubergine
4 medium courgettes
2 medium heads of fennel
2 red peppers
2 yellow peppers
4 'banana' shallots or 12 small shallots
approximately 8 tbsp olive oil
fine sea salt and freshly ground black pepper

To finish the salad
1 bunch basil, leaves torn
50g Parmesan shavings
1 tbsp pinenuts, toasted

To prepare the vegetables Slice the green stem off the aubergines, cut in half lengthways and into 1¹/₂cm thick half-moons. Top and tail the courgettes, slice in half lengthways and then on the angle into 2cm wide pieces.

Cut the fennel heads as described in the method of the fennel recipe on page 146. Cut the peppers in half through the stem and remove the stem and seeds. Cut into 4–5cm squares and slice out any white pith. Peel the shallots, retaining the hairy root. Cut into quarters through the root, so that the layers hold together. Each vegetable will have to be roasted or barbecued separately, as they cook at different rates. Brush the aubergines with olive oil. Toss the other vegetables with the remaining oil; just enough for a light coating. Season well with salt and pepper.

To roast in a wood-fired oven Light your oven according to the instructions on page 24. You will have two oven trays on the go at any time; one on the base and the other on the trivet. The base is slightly cooler. Roast the peppers and courgettes on the trivet and the fennel and shallots on the base. Roast the aubergines wherever space comes first available. As the vegetables become beautifully browned and softened, tip them into your serving bowl. Each tray will take 5–10 minutes. Timings vary immensely; just stay with your oven.

This recipe alone is reason to invest in a wood-fired oven.

Barbecue Preheat the grill and hinged sandwich racks to medium–high or 'sizzle' temperature. Clean and lightly oil the rack. Place the vegetables into the hinged sandwich racks and grill on both sides for approximately 6-7 minutes, turning from time to time. Courgettes may cook a little quicker. Vegetable flesh must be browned before you attempt to move them from the rack: try too early and it will stick. When lightly charred and softened, using a fish slice, remove the vegetables from the rack and transfer to the serving dish.

To serve Toss the wood-roasted vegetables together with the torn basil leaves. Scatter with Parmesan shavings and toasted pinenuts. Serve warm or at room temperature, but never straight out of the fridge.

Tips Roasted vegetables keep well in the fridge for a couple of days and make a great addition to salads, pasta sauces and sandwiches, so make extra if you have the space and the time.

SALAD AND VEGETABLE
ACCOMPANIMENTS

New and Sweet Potatoes with Thyme and Caramelised Red Onions, with Grainy Mustard Dressing

SERVES 6

• At Blistering, we wood-roast the sweet potatoes and the red onions to pack in the flavour. It really is worth your while sparking up the oven.
Or you could parboil them and finish them off on the barbecue. Here we stick to the conventional oven, on the assumption that you have a battery of other barbecued dishes to think about.

500g new potatoes, scrubbed
500g orange sweet potatoes, scrubbed
2tbsp olive oil
3 tsp chopped soft thyme
sea salt and freshly ground black pepper
3 medium red onions
1 tsp sugar
1 recipe quantity Grainy Mustard Dressing
  (see page 177)
3 tbsp flat leaf parsley, roughly chopped

To cook the new potatoes Boil the new potatoes in plenty of boiling salted water for 20 minutes, or until tender. Drain and leave to cool naturally.

To roast the sweet potatoes and the red onions
Preheat the oven to 200C. Wash and cut the sweet potatoes into 2.5cm dice. Don't peel them as the baked skin is very good to eat. Toss the pieces in a bowl with 1 tbsp of the olive oil, half of the chopped thyme and season well with salt and pepper. Transfer to an oven tray, large enough to accommodate the sweet potato in one layer. Use two trays if necessary. Roast in the oven for 20-25 minutes, or until golden brown. Peel and slice the red onions in half. Chop off and discard the hairy root and slice the onion into 1cm squares. Toss in the same bowl with the remaining tablespoon of olive oil, the other half of the thyme, the sugar and season with salt and pepper. Transfer to a non-reactive oven tray and roast for 15-20 minutes, or until caramelised and softened.

To serve While they are still warm, cut the new potatoes down to bite-size if necessary and toss them in a bowl with the Grainy Mustard Dressing and the parsley. The new potatoes absorb the flavour of the vinaigrette so much better while still above room temperature. When the sweet potatoes and onions have cooled, gently mix them in with the new potatoes.

Wood-roast Potatoes

• If you have the oven on for anything, don't miss out on this experience. Here we use goose fat (*see* the Christmas Goose recipe on page 86), but you could use a mixture of olive oil and butter.

1.5kg non-waxy potatoes, such as King Edwards
1tsp sea salt
6 tbsp goose fat
sea salt and freshly ground black pepper

Peel and cut the potatoes into 4–5cm chunks. Place in a large pan and cover with water. Add the salt and bring to the boil. Simmer for 10-12 minutes, or until *al dente*, or not quite cooked through. Drain the potatoes thoroughly in a colander and allow water to evaporate off them.

Heat the goose fat in a roasting tin. Place the *al dente* potatoes into the tin, turning them to coat all surfaces with goose fat. Season well with salt and pepper.

To roast in the wood-fired oven Light the oven. Start the roasting process in the hottest part of the oven i.e. on the trivet. Once the potatoes begin to take some colour, move the roasting tin to the base of the oven. Continue to roast the potatoes, turning the tin through 180 degrees every 7 minutes or so. You should also turn the individual chunks of potato after 20 minutes or so to achieve even all over cooking. Roast for a total of 45 minutes, or until crispy and golden. You may need to give them a final burst of heat on the trivet for that extra golden brown finish.

One of the best ways to cook potatoes.

Vibrant Persian Rice Salad with Nuts, Pomegranate, Dried Fruits and Herbs

SERVES 6

- At Blistering, we don't dress our rice salads, as the flavours speak for themselves and there are so many sauces and juices around on the Blistering buffet for the rice to absorb.
- Yes, we know basmati is an Indian rice, but it has such a great flavour and its grains keep beautifully separate. Vary the ingredients according to what you have in your kitchen cupboards.

150g basmati or other long grain rice
75g wild rice or red Camargue rice
2 tbsp pine nuts
2 tbsp pistachios or pecans
2 tbsp flaked almonds
75g sultanas
75g dried apricots or dates, finely chopped
Seeds of 2 pomegranates, pith removed
4 spring onions, finely sliced
3 tbsp chopped flat leaf parsley
2 tbsp chopped coriander
2 tsp sumac powder (if available)
zest of two lemons
sea salt and freshly ground black pepper

Cook the rices Cook the rices in separate pans of boiling salted water according to the instructions on their packaging. Take care not to overcook, as this salad does not take well to sticky starchy rice. Drain the rices and refresh them under cold running water until cold.

To serve Heat a dry frying pan or skillet. Add the nuts and toast, shaking from time to time to prevent burning. Mix the rices with all the other salad ingredients, seasoning to taste with salt and pepper.

Jamaican Rice and Peas

SERVES 6

- The peas in this traditional Jamaican hot rice dish are not the green peas we know, but dried beans. Dried beans are a must for this dish, as cooking liquor is used to boil the rice. This side dish is an essential with the Jerked Rack of Ribs (page 108), or Jerked Chicken thighs.
- Rice in general can be tricky to cook, but not in this recipe, where starchiness is seen as a virtue. It's like a simple Jamaican Paella. We like to use two varieties of beans
- Soak the beans overnight

For the 'peas'
100g dried black-eyed beans
100g black beans
1 stick celery, washed and cut in half
1 medium onion, peeled and cut in half
1 large carrot, peeled and cut in half
2 cloves garlic, peeled
2 bay leaves
6 sprigs fresh thyme, divided in two

1 tbsp vegetable oil
1 medium onion, finely chopped
3 cloves garlic, finely chopped
1 large mild red chilli, deseeded and finely chopped, or to taste
1 large mild green chilli, deseeded and finely chopped, or to taste
$1/2$ tsp ground allspice
350g American long grain rice
1.2 litres beans cooking liquor
1 tsp fine sea salt
$1/4$ tsp freshly ground black pepper
6 spring onions, finely chopped
2 tbsp roughly chopped coriander

Soak the beans overnight in two separate bowls. After soaking, drain them separately through a colander, wash them and then drain again. Place the two bean varieties in two separate saucepans, dividing the vegetables between the two. Cover with cold water to 5cm above the level of the beans and vegetables. Don't add salt, as salt toughens the skins of the boiling beans. Bring to the boil, skimming off any scum with a ladle. Simmer for 20-25 minutes, or until cooked. Black beans take a little longer than black-eyed beans. Strain, retaining the cooking liquor. Pick out and discard the vegetables and herbs.

Heat the oil in a heavy-bottomed pan on a medium heat. Add the onion and garlic and cook for 2-3 minutes. Add the chilli, allspice and rice to the pan and cook gently, stirring for a further 3-4 minutes, or until the rice is translucent. Taking care to avoid a steam burn, add the beans cooking liquor to the rice. Add the salt and pepper. Stir, bring to the boil and simmer for 10 minutes. If the rice has absorbed all the liquor at this point, add another couple of ladlefuls of beans cooking liquor. Add the cooked beans and the spring onions and bring back to the simmer. Stir well and turn off the heat. Cover the surface with parchment paper and place on a tightly fitting lid, or stretch over some clingfilm, so that the rice and peas can continue to cook and absorb juices. Leave for 5-7 minutes. Fork up and adjust seasoning.

Turn out the Rice and Peas into a serving bowl and sprinkle with the coriander.

Tips To make a luscious, richer Rice and Peas, replace some of the rice cooking water with half a 400ml can of coconut milk, keeping the same total volume of liquid.

Cous Cous with stacks of Parsley and Mint, Roasted Red Peppers, Lemon and Spring Onion

SERVES 6

- Particularly suitable for Middle Eastern-themed menus.
- Don't chop and add the mint until the last minute – it will blacken.

2 red peppers
1 tbsp olive oil for roasting the peppers
sea salt and freshly ground black pepper
275g cous cous
1 tbsp extra virgin olive oil
juice of 1 medium-sized lemon
equal volume of water to cous cous
$1/2$ tsp salt
$1/2$ tsp freshly ground black pepper
8 spring onions, finely chopped
3 tbsp chopped flat-leaf parsley
2 tbsp chopped mint

To roast the peppers Preheat the oven to 200C. Cut the pepper in half through the stalk. Remove the stem, seeds and pith. Cut each half into three lengthways. Toss with the olive oil and season with salt and pepper. Place in the oven and roast for 25 minutes, or until browning and softened. Remove from the oven, and taking great care, cover the hot tray with clingfilm. The pepper skin will sweat off as they cool. After 20 minutes or so, skin the peppers and slice them into 1cm squares, or into strips as desired.

To prepare the cous cous Weigh the cous cous and tip into a measuring jug, noting the volume of the grains. Transfer to a bowl and toss the grains with the olive oil, lemon juice, $1/4$ tsp salt and plenty of freshly ground pepper. Have some clingfilm at the ready and bring a kettle of water to the boil. Measure out the same volume of boiling water as there was cous cous and pour immediately over the grains. Stir once and cover immediately with clingfilm. Leave to soak for 4 minutes, remove the clingfilm, fork up the grains and cover again. Leave for a further 2 minutes. Tip onto a tray and break up any lumps. Leave to cool.

To serve Mix the cous cous with the red peppers, spring onions and chopped parsley. Chop and add the mint at the last minute. Adjust the seasoning to taste.

A great change from rice, cous cous is fantastic with either hot or cold dishes.

Oriental Spicy Egg Noodle Salad

SERVES 6

- This salad goes terrifically well with any Asian or oriental main course dish. The dressed noodles sit happily in the fridge overnight, but don't stir in the vegetables until you are ready to serve.
- You could use the egg noodle nests readily available from all supermarkets. We buy the finer pre-steamed variety from oriental supermarkets, which require no cooking; only soaking. We find that they are less likely to become starchy and sticky.

1 x 250g pack fine egg noodles
1 tbsp sesame oil
225g sugar snap peas, topped and de-stringed
1/2 cucumber
200g bean sprouts
8 spring onions, washed, trimmed and finely sliced on the diagonal
1 red pepper, deseeded and finely sliced
1 yellow pepper, deseeded and finely sliced
4 tbsp chopped fresh coriander
2 large mild chillies, deseeded and finely chopped

For the dressing
3 tsp sesame seeds
2 tsp blue poppy seeds
3 tbsp soy sauce
1 tbsp runny honey
2 tbsp rice vinegar
2 tsp fish sauce

For the noodles Prepare the noodles following the instructions on the pack. Transfer to the serving bowl and toss with the sesame oil.

Prepare the vegetables Bring a large pan of salted water to the boil. Blanch the sugar snap peas for no more than 45 seconds, drain and refresh in ice-cold water. Slice the cucumber in four lengthways. Slice out the seeds and cut the cucumber thinly on an angle. Combine with all the remaining salad ingredients and the noodles in the serving bowl.

Prepare the dressing Toast the sesame and poppy seeds in a dry skillet or frying pan, holding a lid over the top to stop them from escaping as they pop. Mix the soy sauce, honey, rice vinegar and fish sauce with the seeds.

To serve Mix together all the ingredients.

As much a vegetable salad as a noodle salad – full of colour and crunch.

Chickpeas, Black Beans and Broad Beans with Artichokes, Red Onions, Red Peppers and Tarragon Dressing

SERVES 6

- Colourful, bright and summery and goes with anything, this one will keep both vegetarians and meat eaters more than happy. Do make the effort to soak dried pulses, rather than resorting to the tinned variety. Tinned pulses make a really poor second.
- Soak the beans overnight or for 24 hours

100g dried black beans, soaked overnight
100g dried chickpeas, soaked overnight
3 tbsp extra virgin olive oil
2 cloves garlic, finely chopped
2 mild red chillies, deseeded and finely chopped
juice of 1 lemon
1 tsp sea salt
1/2 tsp freshly ground black pepper
200g shelled broad beans – frozen are fine if you can't get fresh
250g tinned artichoke hearts, or baby artichokes in oil
1/2 medium red onion, peeled and finely sliced
1 large red pepper, diced
2 tbsp chopped tarragon

For the pulses Place the black beans and chickpeas in two separate pans. Cover with cold water to 5cm above the level of the beans. Bring both pans to the boil, boiling rapidly for the first 10 minutes, skimming off any scum that develops and then simmering for a further 10-15 minutes for the black beans and a further 30-40 minutes for the chickpeas, or until tender. Do not add salt to the water, as this will only serve to toughen their skins. Drain well.

Dress the pulses Mix the oil with the garlic, chilli, lemon juice, salt and pepper. Mix this dressing with the drained pulses while they are still warm, allowing the flavours to infuse as the pulses cool.

Prepare the other ingredients Bring a pan of salted water to a rolling boil. Add the broad beans, bring back to the boil and blanch for 1 minute. Drain through a colander and refresh with ice-cold water. Cut the artichoke hearts into bite-size pieces.

To serve Mix together all the ingredients. Toss well and serve. If you are making up the salad in advance, keep the dressed pulses separate from the other ingredients until the last minute. Take out of the fridge at least one hour before serving.

Colourful, bright and summery – and goes with anything.

Puy Lentils, Feta, Red Onions and Semi-dried Tomatoes with Thyme and Raspberry Vinaigrette

SERVES 6

- Puy lentils are the best of their kind. They have a great colour and mellow flavour and won't break down to mush once cooked.
- At Blistering, we semi-dry our own tomatoes in a slow conventional oven overnight, but you can buy them at the deli counter as 'Sunblush' tomatoes.

For the dressing
$1/2$ red onion, peeled, halved and very finely sliced or diced
75g semi-dried or 'Sunblush' tomatoes, drained and roughly chopped
2 tsp chopped thyme leaves
$1^1/2$ tbsp raspberry vinegar
4 tbsp extra virgin olive oil
sea salt and freshly ground black pepper

200g Puy lentils, washed and picked through for stones
1 bay leaf
3 sprigs thyme
110g feta cheese, cubed or crumbled

Prepare the dressing Combine the dressing ingredients in a bowl, seasoning with salt and pepper to taste.

To cook the lentils Place the lentils, bay leaf and thyme sprigs in a saucepan and cover with water so that the water level is 2.5cm higher than the lentils. Do not add salt. Bring to the boil and simmer for around 20 minutes, or until the lentils are tender. Cooking time will vary with, amongst other factors, the age of the lentils. Drain the lentils well and spread them on a non-reactive tray. Pick out the bay leaf and thyme sprigs.

To finish the salad While still warm, pour the dressing over the lentils, distributing the flavours by stirring with a wooden spoon. Once cool, transfer to a serving bowl and toss with feta cheese. Check for seasoning.

Thai Salad with Green Papaya, Spring Onions, Red Peppers and Green Beans

SERVES 6

- There is a lot going on in this salad. It's crunchy, hot, sour, salty and sweet all at the same time. A classic Thai accompaniment, though spicy, it is cooling and above all very addictive.
- Green papaya and all the dressing ingredients are available from oriental stores. Green papaya is an extremely hard vegetable, so you will need a Japanese or a standard mandolin, or the thick grater on a food processor to shred it. If you can't get hold of the green papaya, track down some hard under-ripe orange papaya – you're going for a firm crunch.

450g green papaya
225g fine green beans, topped and tailed
6 spring onions, washed, trimmed and finely sliced on the diagonal
1 red pepper, deseeded, pith removed and finely sliced
2 tbsp roughly chopped fresh coriander

For the dressing
3 tbsp sugar stock syrup (*see* below)
4 tbsp fish sauce (nam pla)
2 tsp ground dried shrimp
juice of 2 limes
2 Thai 'birdseye' chillies, finely chopped or 1 tsp dried chilli flakes, or to taste
1 small clove garlic, finely chopped

To serve
1 tbsp ground peanuts (optional)

To prepare the vegetables Peel the papaya and cut it in half lengthways. Remove the shiny black seeds. Matchstick the papaya on the mandolin. Blanch the beans in boiling salted water for 2 minutes and refresh in ice-cold water. Drain and mix all the prepared vegetables and coriander together in a bowl.

To make sugar stock syrup This is a thick syrup, which has many purposes. Place 1kg sugar with 650ml of water in a pan. Dissolve slowly over a low heat. Do not allow the syrup to boil until all the sugar is dissolved. Simmer for 5 minutes. Set aside and leave to cool. Transfer to a sterilised jar. Keep it in the fridge.

To prepare the salad Mix together the dressing ingredients in a bowl or jug. Pour the dressing over the vegetables and coriander and mix well with a wooden spoon. The Thais would use a large pestle and mortar, crushing the flavours of the dressing into the vegetables – you could do something similar in a bowl with the end of a wooden rolling pin or with a wooden spoon. Cover and refrigerate for at least half an hour, to really get the flavours going.

To serve Transfer the salad to a serving platter and sprinkle with peanuts if you like.

Sweet and Sour Slaw with Sesame, Chinese Leaves, Bean Sprouts, Peppers, Spring Onions and Fresh Pineapple

SERVES 6

- A Blistering favourite that goes wonderfully with sausages and burgers.
- If you can get hold of different varieties of sprouted beans from a speciality store (e.g. sprouted chick peas, moong beans, etc.), then all the better.

1/2 head (a dozen or so leaves) of Chinese Leaves, leaves separated, washed and dried
1 red pepper
1/2 yellow pepper
8 spring onions
1/2 small ripe sweet pineapple
150g bean sprouts, or sprouted bean varieties
1 tbsp toasted sesame seeds
3 tbsp chopped coriander

For the dressing
3/4 tbsp tomato ketchup
3/4 tbsp sesame oil
3/4 tbsp rice vinegar
1 heaped tsp sugar
1/4 tsp dried chilli flakes, or to taste (optional)

To prepare the vegetables and fruit Bunch together the Chinese leaves and slice across them thinly. Cut the peppers in half through the stalk and then again into quarters. Remove the stem, seeds and pith and slice the peppers thinly. Trim the spring onions and slice them on a sharp diagonal. Cut the skin off the pineapple, cutting out any eyes once you have done so. Cut into four, straight down through the hard core. Cut the core out of the four pieces and discard. Slice across the pineapple into wafer-thin slices. Mix all the salad ingredients together with the pineapple.

To prepare the salad Combine the dressing ingredients in a bowl. Pour the dressing over the salad and toss well. Serve straight away or it will wilt.

A very simple-to-make, bright and very tasty summer salad that everyone will love.

Crunchy Carrot Salad with Mustard Seeds, Pumpkin Seeds, Sunflower Seeds, Pinenuts and a Sweet Lemon Dressing

SERVES 6

- We just love this salad – and it's so good for you. Everyone asks for the recipe. Now we can tell them to buy the book.
- Can be made a day ahead.

450g carrots
1 tbsp pine nuts
1 tbsp sunflower seeds
1 tbsp pumpkin seeds
$1/2$ tbsp black mustard seeds
$1/2$ tbsp sesame seeds

For the dressing
juice of 1 large lemon
2 tbsp stock sugar syrup (*see* first part of marinade instructions on page 76)
1 tsp sea salt
$1/2$ tsp freshly ground black pepper

Top, tail and peel the carrots. Either matchstick them on a mandolin or if your knife skills are up to it, with a sharp kitchen knife. Alternatively grate coarsely. Transfer to a mixing bowl.

Mix together the pine nuts, sunflower seeds and pumpkin seeds in a bowl. Heat a large frying pan or skillet on the hob for a few minutes and tip in the contents of the bowl. Toast for a minute or two, shaking the pan to avoid burning, or until just beginning to pick up colour. Add the mustard and sesame seeds to the pan and continue to toast, shaking every 15 seconds or so, until the seeds are nicely toasted and aromatic. Remove from the heat and tip immediately over the carrots, stirring them in with a 'tssss'.

Combine the dressing ingredients in a bowl or mug and tip them over the carrots and seeds. Stir well. This salad is best made at least an hour before serving. So cover it and refrigerate.

Vivid Green Salad with Fine Green Beans, Sugar Snap Peas, Mangetouts and Cucumber dressed with Lime, Rice Vinegar and Coriander

SERVES 6

- Rather than defaulting to the standard green leaf salad, try this crunchy fresh emerald-bright salad for a change. Dress the salad at the last minute to prevent discolouration of the beans.
- You're best using a 'spider' to fish the blanched vegetables out of the pan, otherwise use a slotted spoon or small sieve.

150g fine green beans
150g sugarsnap peas
110g mangetouts
1/2 cucumber
3 tbsp chopped coriander

For the dressing
juice of 1 lime
2 tsp rice vinegar
1 tbsp stock sugar syrup (*see* first part of marinade instructions on page 76)
1 heaped tsp toasted sesame seeds
1/2 tbsp chopped fresh mint
sea salt and freshly ground black pepper

To blanch the beans and peas Top and tail the beans, sugarsnap peas and mangetouts. Set a large pan of boiling salted water on the hob and bring to the rolling boil. Set up a colander and a large bowl in the sink for refreshing the blanched vegetables. Plunge the beans in the boiling water and blanch for around 3 minutes, or until when bitten they are just losing their squeak. Using the spider, or sieve, fish out the beans into the bowl and cool the beans immediately under lots of cold tap water. Once cold, strain through the colander. Bring the water back to the boil and repeat the process, but for one minute only with the sugarsnap peas, adding the cooled peas to the colander. Repeat with the mangetouts, but for 30 seconds only. Dry the vegetables well and transfer to the serving bowl.

Slice the cucumber into four lengthways and cut out the seeds. Cut the cucumber quarters into 'quills' about 1/2cm thick on a sharp diagonal. Add to the beans with the chopped coriander.

Combine the dressing ingredients in a bowl or mug and tip them over the vegetables. Stir well and season to taste. Serve within an hour before the acid of the lime and rice vinegar begins to discolour the beans.

A zingy, crunchy green salad without any big flappy leaves.

Creole Slaw with Red and White Cabbage, Celeriac, Green Peppers, Spring Onions and Radishes and Parsley Mayonnaise

SERVES 6

• To accompany Caribbean dishes.

175g red cabbage
175g white cabbage
110g celeriac
1 green pepper
8 spring onions
12 radishes
3 tbsp Hot Horseradish & Parsley Mayonnaise
  (*see* page 177)
extra grated horseradish or horseradish cream,
  to taste
sea salt and freshly ground black pepper
3 tbsp picked parsley leaves

To prepare the vegetables Core, and using a sharp heavy kitchen knife, or the fine slicing blade of a food processor, finely slice the red and white cabbage. Peel and grate the celeriac. Slice the green pepper in half through the stem. Remove the stem, seeds and pith and slice into fine strips. Slice the radishes finely into rounds. Place all the vegetables together in a bowl.

To prepare the salad Combine the Horseradish Mayonnaise with the vegetables and toss well to distribute it evenly. Add more grated horseradish or horseradish cream to taste. Season to taste. Scatter over the parsley leaves.

Slaw with a tad more oomph.

Yellow and Green Courgette Salad

SERVES 6

- Raw courgettes are transformed when they are sliced very finely on a mandolin, or if your knife-skills are up to it, match-sticked with a sharp knife. Here, bright yellow and green and tossed with a sharp herby dressing. They look great and make a simple, refreshing and light salad. Pick small courgettes if possible as the smaller they are, the firmer they are.

250g yellow courgettes
250g green courgettes
1 small bunch flat leaf parsley
1 tbsp vegetable oil
1 level tbsp black mustard seeds

For the dressing
juice of ½ lemon
juice of 1 lime
1 tbsp extra virgin olive oil
1 tsp sugar
sea salt and freshly ground pepper to taste

To prepare the courgettes and parsley
Wash, top and tail the courgettes. Cut into 5cm pieces. Using either a mandolin, or a sharp kitchen knife, slice the courgettes into long thin matchsticks. Transfer to a mixing bowl. Wash and dry the parsley on a towel or in a salad spinner. Pick the leaves, discarding the stalks, and place to one side or in the fridge, wrapped in damp kitchen roll.

To prepare the salad Heat the oil in a frying pan, which has a lid. Pop the mustard seeds in the hot oil, holding on the lid and shaking the pan gently for about 30 seconds, or until you smell the seeds toasting. While still very hot, pour the oil and mustard seeds onto the match-sticked courgettes. For the dressing, mix the lemon and lime juices with the olive oil and sugar in a small bowl. Just before serving, pour the dressing over the courgettes. Add the picked parsley leaves and toss. Season with salt and pepper to taste.

A simple, refreshing light and bright salad.

SAUCES AND RELISHES

Mayonnaise

• Although you can buy some pretty good mayonnaises these days, as a general rule, bought mayonnaises do tend to be a little vinegary. An unctuous glistening mass of homemade mayonnaise is delicious, will not split and is a breeze to make, as long as you follow three simple rules.
i) All ingredients must be at room temperature.
ii) The oil must be added gradually, particularly at the start when each drop must be amalgamated before the next one is added.
iii) Take your time and enjoy the process.
• Oh, and buy only the freshest best quality eggs.

2 freshest egg yolks
1 tsp mild Dijon mustard
2 tsp white wine vinegar or lemon juice
150ml sunflower or groundnut oil
150ml light olive oil
sea salt and freshly ground white pepper, to taste

Mix the egg yolks with the mustard and the vinegar or lemon juice in a large bowl. If there's no one around to hold the bowl for you, fashion a damp tea towel into a ring on your work surface, making a 'nest' for your bowl to sit in. This will stop the bowl from spinning around as you whisk in the oil.

Mix the oils together in a jug. Stirring either with a whisk or a wooden spoon with one hand and pouring from the other, add the oil drop by drop initially, making sure that each drop is amalgamated before adding the next. As the volume of the mayonnaise grows, you'll find that you can increase your pouring rate to a steady trickle. If you find that the mayonnaise is becoming too thick, add a few of drops of water and carry on again.

Once all the oil is added, you will have a shining creamy mass, which you can season to taste. Keeps for a few days covered in the fridge.

Tips If you're scared of raw egg yolks, or are in a hurry, you can mellow out a good quality bought mayonnaise by slowly whisking 50 ml light olive oil into 250ml of bought mayonnaise. You can also buy pasteurised egg yolks in some supermarkets and delicatessens.

Caesar Dressing

• For a great Caesar Salad, just toss ripped cos leaves with this dressing and throw over shards of Parmesan and some croutons. Delicious with anything, but classic with barbecued chicken.

1 or 2 cloves garlic, chopped
a large pinch of fine sea salt
3 salted anchovies
4 tbsp finely grated Parmesan
300ml Mayonnaise (*see above*)
juice of $1/2$ lemon, or to taste
freshly ground white pepper to taste

Place a plate up-side-down on the work surface and put the chopped garlic on its flat underside. Mash it to a paste with the salt using the flat side of a table knife. Chop the anchovies finely. Transfer the garlic paste, anchovies, Parmesan and mayonnaise to a bowl and beat them together. Add the lemon juice to taste. If you use sharper, bought mayonnaise rather than home-made, you may find that you need much less lemon juice, if any. Season with pepper to taste.

Grainy Mustard Dressing

- A favourite for dressing potato salad.

1 tbsp grainy mustard
2 tbsp Mayonnaise (*see* opposite)
6 tbsp extra virgin olive oil
1 tsp red wine vinegar, to taste
sea salt and freshly ground black pepper

Combine the grainy mustard with the mayonnaise in a mixing bowl. Nestle the bowl into a damp tea towel to anchor it down and, using a wire whisk, whisk in the olive oil slowly to prevent splitting. Add the vinegar to taste and season to taste with salt and pepper.

Saffron Aioli

- If you like the taste of saffron, this golden yellow sauce goes brilliantly with chicken, fish or any Middle Eastern dish. You must make it a day in advance in order for the colour and flavour to develop properly.
- Saffron bought in small quantities is terribly expensive. Seek out a good supplier (*see* Suppliers appendix, page 215) and beware of poor imitations.

1 clove garlic, finely chopped
1 tsp saffron threads (approximately 60 strands)
80ml good white wine

300ml Mayonnaise (*see* opposite)
sea salt and freshly ground black pepper

Mix the garlic and saffron with the wine in a small non-reactive saucepan. Place on the heat, bring to the boil and reduce to the volume of half a tablespoon. Take off the heat and leave to cool. Add the unstrained liquid to the mayonnaise. Season with salt and pepper to taste.

Hot Horseradish and Parsley Mayonnaise

- We love to use fresh horseradish root in our Blistering version, but appreciate that it can be tricky to get hold of. It is also an eye-streaming nightmare to grate – horseradish leaves grating onions in the shade. Horseradish creams vary in heat and acidity, so just treat the following as a guide and vary quantities to taste.
- If you are using bought mayonnaise, rather than the less acidic luscious homemade version, then you may choose to reduce or skip on the lemon juice entirely.

2 tbsp hot horseradish cream, or to taste
2 tbsp finely chopped flat-leaf parsley
300ml Mayonnaise (*see* opposite)
$1/4$ tsp cayenne pepper
2 tsp lemon juice, or to taste
sea salt and freshly ground white pepper

Combine the horseradish, parsley, mayonnaise and cayenne. Add lemon juice and seasoning to taste.

Roasted Garlic Mayonnaise

- We love this sauce at Blistering where we make it by the litre. The garlic cloves are slightly caramelised, making for a mellow, sweetish finish. Heaven with anything; even just on toasted ciabatta. When we have our wood-fired oven sparked up, we fill a terracotta tray with cloves of garlic and pour over olive oil and sea salt. We then simply pop it in the oven and the cloves stew in the oil creating great 'confited' garlic and heavenly smoky garlic oil.
- If using bought mayonnaise, make sure you taste it before adding the lime juice, as jarred varieties can be fairly acidic.

12 cloves garlic, skin left on
3 tbsp olive oil
sea salt
300ml Mayonnaise (see page 176)
2 tsp lime juice (optional, but strongly recommended with fish)
freshly ground white pepper to taste

Preheat the oven to 170C. You want the garlic to sit in the oil, pretty much covered, so place the garlic in a tiny tin, or oven-proof dish – something like an individual Yorkshire Pudding tin, a dariole or disposable individual foil pie mould would do. Add the oil and sprinkle over some salt. Bake for 15–20 minutes, or until soft and beginning to caramelise under the skin. Fish the garlic out of the oil with a spoon, putting the oil to one side to cool. You will be using it later. While still warm peel the garlic (the skins will just fall off) and either mash the cloves with a fork, or if you want a smoother texture, push them through a fine sieve with the back of a spoon. Mix the roasted garlic paste with the mayonnaise. When cool, whisk in the oil the garlic was cooked in, adding in a slow dribble to prevent the mayonnaise from splitting. Add lime juice if you want a sharper edge and season with salt and pepper to taste.

Marie Rose Sauce

- So much better made with homemade mayonnaise.

6 tbsp Mayonnaise (see page 176)
1$\frac{1}{2}$ tbsp tomato ketchup
3 tsp Worcestershire Sauce
juice of 1 lemon, or to taste

3 tsp brandy
sea salt and freshly ground white pepper

Spoon the mayonnaise into a bowl. Whisk in the other ingredients, seasoning with salt and pepper to taste.

Wasabi Mayonnaise

- The following recipe is just to act as a guide, as there are a few variables. Firstly, the strength of the horseradish-like wasabi flavour in this sauce is a matter of taste. Secondly, prepared wasabi pastes do vary in strength, depending on brand and age. Lastly, if you use bought mayonnaise instead of making your own, watch the salt and lime juice quantities as the bought versions tend to be quite salty and vinegary already.

6 tbsp Mayonnaise (see page 176)
3 tsp wasabi paste
$\frac{1}{4}$ tsp fine sea salt
3 tsp fresh lime juice

Spoon the mayonnaise into a bowl with the wasabi paste and salt and combine. Gently whisk in the lime juice. Blend well, making sure that you have no green lumps of wasabi.

Hollandaise

- This classic rich buttery sauce makes a great dip for bites and is delicious with beef or fish dishes. The instructions may sound tricky, but once you've had a go and get a feel for it, you'll find it a breeze. You can make the reduction and clarify the butter a day ahead, but you have to make the sauce just before serving, as it doesn't keep well.
- This sauce is cooked in a bain marie, or a bowl over a pan of hot water, so you will need to find a mixing bowl that fits snugly over one of your saucepans.

4 tbsp white wine vinegar
4 parsley stalks
1 bay leaf
20 black peppercorns
3 fresh egg yolks
225g unsalted butter
squeeze of lemon juice (optional, but recommended for fish dishes)
sea salt and freshly ground black pepper

Making the reduction Place the vinegar with the parsley stalks, bay leaf and peppercorns in a small saucepan and reduce down the liquid to the volume of one teaspoon. Take off the heat and add a teaspoon of cold water to stop the evaporation. Take the mixing bowl that fits over your saucepan and strain the reduction into it through a sieve. Add the egg yolks and combine with the reduction.

Clarifying the butter Rinse out the saucepan you used for the reduction and place on a gentle heat. Melt the butter in the pan. Once melted, leave to cook gently until the fats separate from the curds and whey – about 6 minutes. There will be froth on the top and the curds and whey will settle at the bottom of the pan. Skim off the froth and pour the clear bright yellow butter fat off the watery curds into a jug. Discard the residue.

'Cooking out' the eggs You are cooking the egg yolk mixture in a bowl over a pan of hot water – i.e. in a bain marie. But watch out, because if the bowl becomes too hot, the yolks will overcook and scramble. Pour an inch of water into the bain marie saucepan and bring to a bare simmer. Whisk the egg yolk mixture off the heat for 30 seconds to aerate the eggs. Place the bowl over the barely simmering pan of water. Whisk the egg mixture continuously. The mixture froths up and cooks to a creamy shiny finish. This will take around 4-5 minutes. If at any point the water begins to boil, take the eggs off the heat or they will scramble. It's as well to lift the bowl off the pan every 30 seconds or so, still whisking, just to slow things down a little.

Making the sauce Make sure that the melted butter fat is just warm; too hot and the eggs will split. Take the eggs off the heat once cooked. If there is no one around to hold the bowl, fashion a damp tea towel into a ring on your work surface, making a 'nest' for your bowl to sit in. This will stop the bowl from spinning around as you whisk in the butter. Whisking with one hand and pouring with the other, add the warm butter drop by drop initially, making sure that each drop is amalgamated before adding the next. As the volume of the hollandaise grows, you'll find that you can increase your pouring rate to a steady trickle. If the sauce is becoming too thick, add a couple of teaspoons of warm water to let it down and carry on adding the butter. Add lemon juice if you like. Season with salt and pepper to taste. Serve immediately, or keep warm over hot water, stirring from time to time.

Garlic Yoghurt Sauce

- Very simple and an essential drizzle on a kebab. This recipe should be enough to spoon over four Lamb Shwarma Kebabs (*see* page 55). Best made a day in advance.

1 small clove garlic, chopped
generous pinch of salt
150ml natural yoghurt
1 tsp lemon juice

1 tbsp water
sea salt and freshly ground white pepper to taste

Place a plate, up-side-down on the work surface. Place the chopped garlic and salt on its flat underside and mash it to a paste using the flat side of an ordinary table knife.
Mix together with all the other ingredients. Season to taste with salt and pepper.

Béarnaise

- This sauce, which is tailor-made to go with beef is created using exactly the same principles as hollandaise – just different flavours. Traditional béarnaise also contains a spoon of reduced beef stock, but we keep it straight in case vegetarians want to indulge.

4 tbsp white wine vinegar
1 small shallot, finely chopped
2 sprigs fresh chervil
2 sprigs fresh tarragon
1 bay leaf
20 black peppercorns
3 fresh egg yolks
225g unsalted butter
2 tsp finely chopped chervil
2 tsp finely chopped tarragon
sea salt and freshly ground black pepper

Making the reduction Place the vinegar with the shallot, chervil, tarragon, bay leaf and peppercorns in small saucepan and reduce down the liquid to the volume of one teaspoon. Take off the heat and add 1 teaspoon of cold water to stop rapid evaporation. Take the mixing bowl that fits over your saucepan and strain the reduction into it through a sieve. Add the egg yolks and combine with the reduction.

Clarifying the butter *See* recipe for Hollandaise, opposite.

'Cooking out' the eggs *See* recipe for Hollandaise.

Making the sauce *See* recipe for Hollandaise, but instead of lemon juice, add the chopped chervil and tarragon and season with salt and pepper to taste. Serve immediately, or keep warm over hot water, stirring from time to time.

Salmariglio

- A great punchy drizzle for roast veggies. Also perfect for fish and chicken. If you would like a milder flavour with the same knockout colour, substitute half of the herbs with baby leaf spinach.

6 tbsp fresh oregano or marjoram leaves
1 tsp flaky sea salt or $^1/_2$ tsp fine sea salt
4 tsp lemon juice
4 tbsp extra virgin olive oil
freshly ground black pepper

Pound the oregano or marjoram in a pestle and mortar with the sea salt, until dark in colour and well broken down. Add the lemon juice and combine well. Slowly pour in the olive oil, stirring as you do so. Add a few twists of pepper and set aside for at least $^1/_2$ hour to let the flavours settle. Keeps well for several days in a lidded jar.

Rocket Pesto

- The aim with pesto is to balance the main flavours of the herbs, the garlic, the Parmesan and the pine nuts, so that no one flavour stands out above any of the others. Here rocket adds an extra explosiveness to the mix.
- This is quite a runny pesto, as we like to drizzle it. Cut back on the oil if you want a more sturdy sauce.

1 tbsp pine nuts
1 clove garlic, finely chopped
$^1/_4$ tsp salt
good handful of rocket leaves, thick stems removed
20g pack of basil
2 tbsp finely grated Parmesan
80ml extra virgin olive oil

Heat a dry frying pan or skillet. Add the pine nuts and toast, shaking every 20 seconds or so until spotted with golden brown. Tip into a bowl to prevent any further browning.

Pound the garlic with the salt to a paste in a pestle and mortar. Add the rocket and basil leaves and grind them into the paste. Add the Parmesan and pine nuts and continue to pound to a paste. Dribble in the olive oil until the desired texture is achieved. Test for seasoning. As rocket has such a peppery flavour, no pepper is needed.

Sweet Mustard & Dill Sauce

- Great with salmon, chicken or sausages.

2 tbsp Dijon mustard
$1^1/_2$ tbsp soft brown sugar
2 tbsp chopped fresh dill

Combine the ingredients.

Blistering Sweet & Sticky Barbecue Sauce

- Makes 1.3 litres.
- The secret is out. Here's the recipe you've all been asking for. It also makes a great marinade for red meats, pork and chicken thighs.
- If you can't get hold of tinned chipotle chillies, substitute dried chilli flakes to taste.

2 tbsp vegetable oil
2 large onions, rough dice
2 thumbs fresh ginger, peeled and chopped
8 cloves garlic, chopped
2 tbsp balsamic vinegar
2 tbsp white wine vinegar
1 litre chopped tinned tomatoes
120ml tomato ketchup
4 tbsp Worcestershire Sauce
4 tbsp oyster sauce

110g soft dark sugar
1 smoked chipotle chilli, minced (optional)
3 tsp dried oregano

Heat the oil in a heavy-bottomed stainless steel pan. Sweat off the onions, ginger and garlic for 6-8 minutes on a medium heat, stirring every minute or so. Add the vinegars, bubble up and reduce the juices down to virtually nothing. Add the other ingredients, bring back to the boil, turn the heat down low and simmer gently for approximately 30 minutes or until well reduced, stirring from time to time to prevent sticking. Blend until smooth and decant, hot, into sterilised jars. A stick blender is perfect for the job and is a must-have tool – saves loads of washing up and time. Once cool, keep the sauce in the fridge.

Cranberry & Orange Sauce

250g cranberries
110g white sugar
200ml orange juice
1/4 tsp pepper
1 bay leaf

Combine the ingredients in a non-reactive pan. Bring to the boil and simmer gently for 20-25 minutes. After 15 minutes or so, the berries will begin to soften. Help them to break down by crushing them with the back of a wooden spoon or a stainless steel fork.
Pour into a sterilised jar. Allow to cool and keep refrigerated. Will keep well for a few weeks.

Chilled Coconut, Lime & Coriander Sauce

- This is a very cooling refreshing yoghurt-based dip. Fantastic with Thai Spatchcocked Poussin (see page 76), or any spicy oriental dish.

150ml natural yoghurt
3 tsp fish sauce (nam pla)
1 tsp lime juice
1 tsp stock syrup (see Thai Salad recipe on page 166) or 1 tsp sugar

2 tbsp coconut powder or coconut cream (not coconut milk)
1 large mild red chillies, deseeded and finely diced
1 tbsp finely chopped coriander
1 tbsp finely chopped mint

Combine all the ingredients in a bowl, whisking out any lumps of coconut powder.

Sweet Soy & Pickled Ginger Dip

- A stunning deep dark dipping or spooning sauce with floating multicoloured spices. If you don't have all the spices on your shelves, don't worry; just use what you have.
- This dip keeps in the fridge for days and improves with age.

4 tbsp soy sauce
2 tbsp stock syrup (*see* Thai Salad on page 166)
1 tbsp runny honey
1 tbsp rice vinegar or lime juice
2 tsp vinegar from the pickled ginger jar
5 stars of star anise

1 tbsp pink pickled ginger, shredded
2 'birdseye', or one red chilli, finely chopped into rings
1 stem lemon grass, finely sliced on an angle
2 lime leaves, finely shredded
5 coriander stems, leaves removed, finely chopped

Bring the liquids with the star anise to the simmer in a small saucepan. Take off the heat and allow to cool for 10 minutes before adding the other ingredients. Keeps for days in the refrigerator.

Coconut Curry Dipping Sauce

- You can easily get hold of all the ingredients in any good oriental store. The coconut powder is not desiccated coconut, but a powdered form of coconut milk that dissolves very easily.

1 tsp vegetable oil
1/2 medium onion, chopped
2 cloves garlic, chopped
2 tsp Thai green curry paste
2 stems lemon grass, chopped
3 lime leaves, shredded
100ml water
1 tbsp fish sauce (nam pla)
half a 400ml can of coconut milk
4 tbsp coconut powder

1 tbsp chopped fresh coriander

Heat the oil in a small saucepan. Add the onion and garlic and sweat on a medium heat for 4-5 minutes, stirring from time to time, until softened and developing a golden colour. Add the Thai green curry paste with the lemon grass and lime leaves and continue to cook, stirring for a further minute. Add the water, fish sauce and coconut milk and bring to the boil. Simmer for 3 minutes. Strain through a sieve and discard the sieve contents. Whisk in the coconut powder and stir in the chopped coriander.

Thai Lime Chilli & Coriander Syrup

- This is a really pretty dip, shown off to full advantage if served in a small glass bowl.

3 juicy limes
80ml stock syrup (see Thai Salad recipe, page 166)
2 tbsp fish sauce (nam pla)
5 stars of star anise
2 small knobs fresh ginger, finely sliced into rounds
1 red birdseye, or one red chilli, finely chopped into rings
1 green birdseye, or one green chilli, finely chopped into rings
1 stem lemon grass, finely sliced on an angle
2 lime leaves, finely shredded
3 coriander stems, finely chopped
7-8 picked coriander leaves

If you have a zester, which takes strips of zest off a lime, use this. Otherwise, use a potato peeler to take off the skin, pare off the pith with a sharp knife and finely shred the zest of one of the limes.

Juice all three limes into a small saucepan and add the stock syrup, fish sauce and star anise. Bring to the boil and turn off the heat before adding all the other ingredients with the exception of the coriander leaves. Leave to cool. Mix in the chopped coriander leaves. Tip the dip into a serving bowl and float the individual leaves just before you serve it. Keeps for days in the refrigerator.

Coriander & Ginger Pesto

- Coriander varies very much in strength (*see* the rant below). We love its sharp aromatic taste and find that it cuts the charred flavour of barbecued food brilliantly – others find it too overbearing. Taking these variables into account, adjust the recipe quantity as appropriate.

1 thumb ginger, peeled and chopped
1 clove garlic
5 tbsp chopped coriander
1 small handful baby spinach leaves, roughly chopped
1 tsp toasted pinenuts
1 level tsp sugar
3 tsp freshly squeezed lemon juice
2 tbsp extra virgin olive oil
sea salt and freshly ground black pepper

Using a blender, whiz the ginger with the garlic. Add the coriander, spinach, toasted pinenuts, sugar and lemon juice and blend for 10 seconds. Slowly drizzle in the olive oil. Season to taste with salt and pepper.

The Coriander Rant
Bunches of pre-packed coriander from supermarkets can be a poor imitation of the Real McCoy. When it's forced under lights, it can have astonishingly little flavour.
The real stuff has strong stalks, white root ends and a bit of dirt to rub and wash off. It really is worth the effort to find this herb in your local Asian market. You get six times for your money and six times the flavour – that's 36 times better.

Blistering Sweet Chilli Sauce

- Makes approximately 600ml
- We use this jewel-bright sauce on pretty much every job we do. If you have a spicy sweet tooth, it's great with pretty much anything.

500g sugar
600ml water
3 cloves garlic, peeled
1 thumb ginger, peeled
8 large red chillies
3 tbsp fish sauce (nam pla)
1 x 410g can chopped tomatoes
dried chilli flakes, to taste

Place the sugar and water in a pan. Dissolve slowly over a low heat. Do not allow the syrup to boil until all the sugar is dissolved.

Simmer for 5 minutes

Roughly chop the garlic and ginger. Cut off and discard the green part of the chillies and slice the chillies in four lengthways. Chop thinly, seeds and all. Pour the syrup into a pan with the fish sauce and tinned tomatoes. Add the ginger, garlic and chilli and bring to the boil. Simmer on a medium heat for about 30 minutes to reduce the volume approximately by half. The sauce will thicken to a sticky shiny syrupy consistency that coats the back of a spoon. If you want more kick, add some dried chilli flakes. If you want a smooth sauce blend it in a food processor, or ideally with a stick blender.

Pour into sterilised jars and leave to cool.

Asian Top Shelf Sauce

• Great sauce, great baste and great marinade for any meat. This is Top Shelf at its best. No fresh ingredients at all – it's like making up a witch's brew. Will keep for weeks in a jar on your kitchen shelf.

150ml oyster sauce
3 tbsp plum sauce
1 tbsp soy sauce
1 tbsp fish sauce (nam pla)
4 tbsp runny honey
2 tsp sugar
1 tbsp sesame oil
1 tbsp rice vinegar
$1/2$ tsp dried chilli flakes
2 tsp dried shrimp, ground (optional)
6 stars of star anise (optional)
2 tsp coriander seeds
1 tbsp sesame seeds
2 tbsp vegetable oil
2 tbsp white mustard seeds

2 tbsp black mustard seeds

Mix together all the sauces, the honey, sugar, sesame oil, rice vinegar, chilli flakes, dried shrimp and star anise in a large bowl.

Heat a dry skillet or frying pan on the hob and toast the coriander seeds, shaking, for around 2 minutes, or until aromatic. Transfer to a spice grinder and blitz for 5 seconds, just to grind to flakes, not to a powder. Tip directly into the sauce. Reheat the skillet and toast the sesame seeds, shaking for 1-2 minutes, or until beginning to pick up colour. Add hot to the sauce. Heat the vegetable oil in the skillet and add the mustard seeds. Allow to sizzle for 1-2 minutes, shaking the pan gently, holding a lid or tray over the top to prevent any hot seeds from popping out of the pan. Tip directly, hot, into the sauce. Mix it all up.

Hummus

• If you're going to the trouble of making your own hummus, go that extra inch and soak and boil dried chickpeas. There is such a difference.
• These quantities are a guide – vary them to taste.

100g dried chickpeas or 1 x 205g can chickpeas, drained and rinsed
1 tbsp tahini
1 cloves garlic, finely chopped
juice of $1/2$ lemon
2 tbsp extra virgin olive oil
sea salt and freshly ground black pepper

Soak the chickpeas for 24 hours or overnight at least. Drain and place in a large saucepan.

Cover the chickpeas with plenty of unsalted water. Bring to the boil and boil vigorously for 10 minutes, then turn down the heat and simmer for 30-40 minutes, or until the chickpeas are cooked. Take off the heat and drain through a colander. Tip the chickpeas onto a tray to cool.

Whilst still warm, transfer the chickpeas to a food processor. Add the tahini, chopped garlic and lemon juice and process until smooth. Carry on processing while you pour in the olive oil in a thin stream. Once the oil is added, if you want a slacker texture, first taste to see if you think it needs more lemon juice. If not, then loosen the hummus with a little water. Season to taste with salt and pepper.

Mint Mojo

- Emerald green, sweet tangy and minty. Great on a lamb burger. Mint jelly is a magical Top Shelf ingredient. Don't be tempted to substitute with mint sauce from a jar.

4 tbsp mint jelly
2 tsp sugar
2 tbsp red wine vinegar
4 tbsp finely chopped mint (one entire 20g sachet of supermarket mint)

1/2 large mild green chilli, finely diced
1 small clove garlic, finely chopped
4 tbsp olive oil
sea salt and freshly ground black pepper to taste

Melt the mint jelly and sugar with the vinegar in a small saucepan, whisking to break up the jelly. Leave to cool. Add the mint, chilli and garlic and slowly blend in the olive oil. Season with salt and pepper to taste.

Sour Cream & Chives

300ml sour cream
4 tbsp finely chopped chives
sea salt and freshly ground black pepper, to taste

Bob's your uncle!

Guacamole

2 medium sized ripe avocados, any bruising removed
1/2 tsp salt
juice 2 small limes
1/2 clove garlic
1/2 small red onion, finely diced
handful of fresh coriander, chopped
1 fresh red chilli, finely chopped

If ripe enough, mash the avocado with a fork along with the salt and lime juice. Otherwise, you will need to dice it finely and toss in the lime juice with the salt. Combine with the other ingredients. Make no more than 6 hours before serving. If not using immediately, cover closely with clingfilm and refrigerate.

Pineapple Pepper & Chilli Salsa

1/4 of a cucumber
1/2 green pepper
1 spring onion
1 large mild red chilli, or to taste
1/4 of a ripe sweet pineapple
2 tsp fish sauce
zest and juice of 1 lime
2 tsp sugar

1 tbsp chopped mint
sea salt and freshly ground black pepper

Slice the cucumber into four lengthways. Slice out the seeds. Finely dice the flesh and transfer to a bowl. Remove the stem, seeds and pith from the pepper and dice finely.

Add to the cucumber. Slice the spring onion on a fine diagonal and deseed and finely dice the red chilli and add both to the mix. Finally, slice off the pineapple skin and dig out any eyes with the point of a knife. Cut the flesh into four equal segments through the hard core. Cut out the core and finely dice the flesh. Transfer the dice with any juices to the bowl. Mix in all the other ingredients and season to taste with salt and pepper.

Chill and serve.

Mango Papaya & Passion Fruit Salsa

• Fruity, light, colourful and tangy. It doesn't matter how ropey your knife skills are – this salsa will always look and taste fantastic. Eat within a couple of hours of making, or it will turn mushy.

1 ripe mango
1 ripe papaya
2 small passion fruits
juice of 1/2 lime
2 spring onions, washed and finely chopped
1 tbsp finely chopped fresh coriander
1 tbsp finely chopped fresh mint
sea salt and freshly ground black pepper

Peel and finely dice the mango and papaya. Place in a bowl. Halve the passion fruits and scoop the juice and pips into the diced fruits. Toss together with all the other ingredients. Season to taste with salt and pepper.

Chill and serve within an hour.

Mango, Lime, Red Onion & Mint Salsa

• Very simple, but very refreshing and delicious with fish, chicken or meat.

1 large ripe mango
1/2 red onion, peeled and finely diced
2 tbsp chopped mint
1 large red chilli, finely diced
2 tsp sugar
1 tsp mint jelly
1 tbsp olive oil

juice of 1 small lime
sea salt and freshly ground black pepper

Peel and dice the mango. Mix together all the ingredients and season to taste with salt and pepper.

Chill and serve.

'Sunblush' Tomato Pesto

100g drained 'Sunblush' or semi-dried tomatoes
1 clove garlic
10g toasted pinenuts
10g freshly grated Parmesan
2 tbsp olive oil
pepper to taste

Blend all ingredients together in a food processor. Store in a sterile airtight jar in the fridge. Can be kept for up to 2 weeks.

Roasted Tomato, Oregano & Red Onion Salsa

• Both delicious and devastatingly pretty. Use any soft herb that is in flower.

450g ripe plum, cherry, 'vine' or beef tomatoes
1 tbsp light olive oil for roasting the tomatoes
sea salt and freshly ground pepper
2 tbsp oregano leaves
oregano flowers (if available)
1/2 raw red onion, finely sliced or diced
1/2 tsp sugar
3 tbsp extra virgin olive oil
2 tsp good quality red wine vinegar

Preheat the oven to 180C. Halve the tomatoes across their equator. Place on an oven tray, drizzle with and toss in the light olive oil. Turn them all cut-side-up, season well with salt and pepper and roast in a medium oven, until soft and slightly coloured. The timing depends on the size of the tomato – about 25 minutes for cherry tomatoes and an hour for beef tomatoes. Allow to cool. If you have used large tomatoes, chop them coarsely. Leave cherry tomatoes as they are. Mix with the other ingredients, seasoning to taste with salt and pepper.

Roughly Chopped Fresh Green Salsa

• A great non-identical twin for the Fresh Tomato Salsa (*see* opposite).
• When choosing herbs to go into a green salsa, use parsley as a base, but don't overdo any of the other herbs; particularly not tarragon, dill or fennel which have powerful flavours.
• How much lime juice and sugar you add depends on the acidity of the capers, the choice of herbs and what you will be serving the salsa with.

3 salted anchovies
1 tbsp drained capers
1 clove garlic
3 tbsp chopped parsley
2 tbsp chopped mixed soft herbs – choose a mix from from chervil, dill, basil, marjoram, fennel and tarragon

4 tbsp extra virgin olive oil
2 spring onions, finely sliced
1/4 cucumber, deseeded and finely diced
2 tsp lime juice, or to taste
1/2 tsp sugar, or to taste
sea salt and freshly ground black pepper

Finely chop the anchovies, capers and garlic. Mix together and pound in a pestle and mortar. Transfer to a bowl and mix in the chopped herbs. Pour in the olive oil, stirring as you go. Add the spring onion and cucumber. Add the lime juice and sugar to taste. Season with salt and pepper.

Fresh Tomato Salsa

• A great multipurpose barbecue favourite. Serve alongside Roughly Chopped Fresh Green Salsa (*see* page 192).

225g ripe plum, cherry or 'vine' tomatoes, diced
1/2 red onion, finely sliced or diced
1/2 tbsp capers, drained and chopped
1/2 red chilli, finely diced

1 tbsp finely torn basil leaves
2 tsp chopped fresh oregano
2 tsp balsamic vinegar
1 tsp sugar
sea salt and freshly ground black pepper

Mix together all the ingredients. Season with salt and pepper.

Shallot & Ginger Relish

• Great with burgers and meats.

2 tbsp vegetable oil
225g shallots, peeled and finely sliced
1 thumb fresh ginger, finely chopped
1 tbsp rice vinegar
1 level tbsp sugar
sea salt and freshly ground black pepper.

Heat the oil in a small saucepan. Sweat the shallots and ginger, stirring from time to time to prevent sticking, for 10 minutes or until well softened and golden. Add the vinegar and sugar and simmer until all the liquid has evaporated. Season to taste.

Store in the refrigerator. Serve at room temperature.

Red Onion Confit

• This is a delicious relish that keeps brilliantly for a couple of weeks in the fridge in a sterilised jar. It has myriad uses – anything from a glamorous burger relish to an accompaniment for venison.
• Note that you must use a stainless steel or non-reactive pan for this recipe – other pans will taint the flavour and colour.

1 tbsp olive oil
450g red onions, finely sliced
1 tsp fresh thyme leaves
1 heaped tbsp soft brown sugar
2 tbsp balsamic vinegar
2 tbsp red wine
1 tsp sea salt and plenty of freshly ground black pepper

Heat the oil in a heavy bottomed stainless steel or non-stick pan. Add the red onions, and cook for 12-15 minutes or until very wilted. Add the thyme and cook for a further 2 minutes. Put in the remaining ingredients and cook very slowly for 30-40 minutes, stirring occasionally to give a shiny sweet caramelised mass of red onions. Transfer to a sterilised jar. Cool and refrigerate.

Minted Mustard Seed & Cucumber Raita

• Cucumber drained for 2 hours before use.

1/2 cucumber, washed, deseeded and coarsely grated
1/2 tsp fine sea salt
1 tbsp black mustard seeds
300ml natural yoghurt
2 tbsp finely chopped fresh mint
sea salt and freshly ground white pepper

Mix the grated cucumber with the salt. The salt will suck excess water out of the cucumber flesh. Transfer to a sieve over a bowl to catch the bright green drips and refrigerate for at least 2 hours. After this time, rinse the salt off the cucumber and press the excess juices through the sieve with the back of a spoon.

Heat a dry frying pan or skillet. Add the mustard seeds and toast, shaking, with the lid on to prevent the seeds from popping everywhere. Tip into the drained cucumber. Mix with the other ingredients. Season to taste with salt and pepper.

Chill and serve.

Salty Onion, Chilli & Lemon Relish

- So simple but this is another of those recipes that produces something that is somehow more than the sum of its parts.
- Leave to mature overnight, or for at least 6 hours.

1 medium onion – white skin is best
1/2 tsp chilli flakes, or to taste
juice of 1 large lemon
1 tsp salt

Peel and halve the onion. Slice the onion paper-thin with a very sharp kitchen knife. Take your time if your knife-skills aren't great; it's important for the flavour and the texture that the onion should be sliced very thinly. Mix the four ingredients together in a small bowl. Pack them down, cover with Clingfilm and place a weight on top if you can. Refrigerate for at least 6 hours, preferable overnight. Serve chilled.

Green Tomato Chutney

- Makes approximately 4.5kg.
- Blistering make gallons of this every summer, laying plenty down for the next year. This is simply the nicest English summer chutney recipe we know.

1.8kg green tomatoes, chopped
700g tart apples, peeled and chopped
450g onions, peeled and chopped
5 cloves garlic, finely chopped
2 thumbs ginger, finely chopped
350g sultanas or chopped dried apricots
50g black mustard seeds
1 tsp chilli flakes, or to taste
110g salt
850ml white wine or cider vinegar
900g soft brown or demerara sugar

Boil up all the ingredients with the exception of the sugar in a large stainless steel pan or jam pan. Simmer for about $1^{1}/_{2}$ hours, or until mushy. Stir from time to time to prevent sticking on the bottom.

Add the sugar, dissolve and simmer for a further 20 minutes.

Wash enough jars and lids in hot soapy water and rinse them well. Dry them totally in a slow oven. Alternatively, sterilise the jars and lids in a large pan of boiling water. Pour the chutney into the hot jars, seal with the lid immediately and label up.

Pomegranate Molasses & Mint Dipping Sauce

1 litre pomegranate juice
2 tsp molasses
1 level tbsp chopped mint

Place the pomegranate juice in a non-reactive saucepan over a high heat. Bring to the boil and reduce down to 100ml. Add the molasses and melt into the reduction. Allow to cool and then add the chopped mint

Green Harissa

- This is a great drizzle for Middle Eastern or simply seasoned barbecue dishes and teams up brilliantly with Middle Eastern Minted Yoghurt (*see* below). If you want a firmer sauce, pull back on the water.
- If you want extra heat, leave the chilli seeds in.

1/2 tsp caraway seeds
1/2 tsp cumin seeds
1/2 tsp coriander seeds
2-3 large mild green chillies, deseeded and chopped, or to taste
1 clove garlic, chopped
1/2 thumb ginger, chopped
50g fresh spinach leaves
2 tbsp chopped fresh coriander
1 tbsp chopped fresh mint
100ml water
2 tbsp olive oil
sea salt and freshly ground black pepper

Heat a dry frying pan or skillet. Add all the seeds and toast for 1-2 minutes, or until aromatic, shaking to prevent scorching. Transfer to the spice grinder and blitz to a powder. Place all the ingredients, except for the olive oil into a blender and blitz until smooth. With the blender still running, dribble in the oil. Season to taste.

Middle Eastern Minted Yoghurt

- Great for cooling down those intense Middle Eastern spices.

300ml Greek, or thick natural yoghurt
3 tbsp chopped fresh mint
sea salt to taste
1/2 tsp sumac powder
2 tsp extra virgin olive oil

Mix the yoghurt with the mint. Season to taste. Transfer to a serving bowl and sprinkle with the sumac powder. Drizzle with the olive oil. Serve chilled.

Refried Beans

- An essential accompaniment to South American dishes.

2 tbsp olive oil
1/2 red onion, finely diced
2 cloves garlic, finely chopped
1/2 tsp ground cumin
410g tin pinto or red kidney beans, drained
80ml water
pinch dried chilli flakes
sea salt and freshly ground black pepper

Heat the olive oil in a frying pan. Add the onions, garlic and cumin and cook for approximately 5 minutes, stirring occasionally until golden brown. Add the drained beans and chilli flakes and mash the beans with the back of a fork. Add 80ml water and stir. Cook the flavours into the beans for 4 minutes, stirring. The beans will look very runny initially, but dry out miraculously. Add more water if necessary. If using in the Mexican Beef Fajita recipe (*see* page 50), the refried beans will act as 'glue' to hold together your finished fajitas, so they need to be thick, but spreadable.

PUDDINGS

Blistering Pavlova – A Glorious Pudding Mountain decorated with Petals, Edible Glitter and Sparklers

SERVES 18-20

- Let the imagination run riot. Meringue, fresh berries and cream decorated however you like. Without a doubt, this spectacular pudding is the Blistering best seller for weddings, birthdays or at any large gathering needing a bit of wow-factor after dinner. It took three of us to carry our biggest one for its grand entrance -for 250 wedding guests.
- The Blistering Pavlova Mountain is made in ever decreasing sized layers, starting with a large round pavlova at the base and topping it with a small meringue 'peak'. The following recipe will serve 20 guests and has five layers.
- The Blistering Pavlova doesn't stand up for hours, so is best assembled just before serving. Thankfully, it is enormous fun to put together; fun that should be shared. Assemble a select few of your most creative guests and create a masterpiece. Make things easy for yourself and bake the meringues, whip the cream and wash and hull the berries where necessary before your guests arrive.
- Make meringues up to 3 days ahead. Store in airtight boxes.

For the meringues
12 egg whites
750g caster sugar
3 tbsp cornflour
scant teaspoon of vanilla essence
3 tsp white wine vinegar

To assemble the pavlova
850ml double or whipping cream
2 tbsp kirsch (optional)
3 punnets strawberries, washed and hulled
3 punnets raspberries
1 punnet blackberries
1 punnet blueberries, washed
4 tbsp runny honey
pink and red edible rose petals
Blistering Edible Glitter
  (*see* www.blistering.co.uk for details) or icing sugar

To make the meringue Preheat the oven to 140C. Use either an electric cake mixer with the whisk attachment, or a handheld electric whisk. Wash the bowl thoroughly with hot soapy water, rinse and dry before whisking the egg whites to stiff peaks. Watch carefully, and beware of over-beating, which gives the meringue a grainy, separated appearance. Mix the caster sugar with the cornflour and add slowly, beating all the time, spoon by spoon. Each time more sugar is added, the egg whites will 'drop' and need to be whipped back up before the addition of the next spoonful. Once all the sugar and cornflour are added, mix in the vanilla essence and the vinegar. Whip for a further 4-5 minutes to bring the mix back up to volume. You will have a sturdy 'marshmallowy' glossy meringue mix. Line your baking trays with baking parchment. The mix will make 5 meringues of decreasing diameters; 25cm, 20cm, 15cm, 10cm and 8cm. This last meringue, the 'peak' is best made with a piping bag. Bake for 1³/₄-2 hours, or when a skewer inserted into the heart of the meringue comes out clean. Cool on wire racks.

To assemble the pavlova Now for the fun part. Whisk the cream to soft peaks and stir in the optional kirsch. Place the largest meringue on a serving plate and spoon over one third of the cream, spreading it right up to the edges. Top with one third of the mixed berries, making sure that you place plenty around the edges where they will be seen when you put on the next layer. Place on the second meringue layer, top with just short of half of the remaining cream and scatter over just short of half of the remaining berries – again right up to the edge. Place on the third and fourth meringue layers, spreading the remaining cream and scattering with berries, retaining some berries for final decoration. Top the pavlova with the meringue 'peak'. Stud the remaining berries onto the protruding cream where you feel there are gaps to be filled. Drizzle the honey slowly off the spoon and allow it to run down the slopes of the pavlova. Either sprinkle with the magical Blistering Edible Glitter, or dust over some icing sugar with a sieve. Scatter with rose petals. They will stick to the honey where they fall. Serve straight away.

Tips For special occasions, light up your pavlova with sparklers or candles.

The Chocoholics' Bar

This is a really fun way to finish any party. Picture a table covered with all things chocolate. Just like an Indian banquet, the more guests you have, the more varieties you can include. Pick and mix from any of the following ideas. You can even accompany this chocoholic's feast with overflowing bowls of your favourite chocolate sweets.

Rich Chocolate Brownies

MAKES 24 TWO BITE-SIZE BROWNIES

40g plain flour
60g cocoa
375g sugar
125g walnuts/pecans
250g good quality dark chocolate
250g unsalted butter
4 eggs, lightly beaten
1 tsp vanilla essence

Preheat the oven to 180C. Line a 20 x 30cm cake tin with baking parchment. Sift the flour and cocoa. Stir in the sugar and the nuts. Using a heavy knife, chop the chocolate finely and add this to the dry ingredients. Melt the butter and allow to cool slightly before combining with the dry ingredients. Stir in the eggs and vanilla essence. Pour into the prepared tin and bake for approximately 35-40 minutes, or until almost firm in the centre.

Chocolate Brandy Polenta Cake

FOR 12 GOOD SLICES

240g good quality dark chocolate
120g butter
5 eggs
150g caster sugar
4 tbsp brandy
120g ground polenta

Preheat the oven to 175C. Butter a loose-based 24cm cake tin. Break up the chocolate and melt with the butter in a double boiler, or in a bowl above a pan of hot water. Don't let the water boil. Separate the eggs and whisk the yolks with the sugar for 3 minutes, or until pale and thick. Allow the melted chocolate-butter mix to cool to just warm before mixing in the beaten egg yolks and sugar, along with the brandy. Whisk the egg whites to peaks and fold into the mixture. Fold in the polenta and transfer the mixture to the cake tin. Bake for around 30 minutes, or until firm to the touch in the centre.

Drown your guests in chocolate!

White and Dark Chocolate Mousse

• The recipe is the same for either mousse.

150g good quality white or dark chocolate
1 egg plus 1 egg yolk
1 tbsp sugar (optional for white chocolate mousse)
325ml double cream
3 tsp spirit – brandy for the dark and Cointreau or
  kirsch for the white

Melt the chocolate in a bowl above a pan of barely simmering water. Scrape the chocolate into another large bowl to cool and wash the original bowl thoroughly. Place the egg, the yolk and sugar in the double boiler and whisk over the heat until they become pale and thick. Do not allow the cooked egg to sit still in the bowl for any time, as it may scramble at the bottom, so keep stirring every minute or so as it cools. Whip the cream to soft peaks in another bowl and stir in the alcohol. When the chocolate has cooled, mix in the eggs and fold the cream.

You can serve the mousses separately. But it's more fun to serve this mousse in glasses; layers of white and dark mousse alternating.

White Chocolate Dip for Strawberries and Cherries

FOR 2 PUNNETS OF STRAWBERRIES OR EQUIVALENT CHERRIES

350ml double cream
450g white chocolate
1/4 tsp vanilla essence
1 tsp lemon juice

Cherries
Strawberries

Bring the cream to the boil in a small saucepan. Watch carefully to stop it from boiling over. Take the pan off the heat and break in the chocolate. Stir until melted. Add the vanilla and the lemon juice and leave to cool. Serve with bowls of cherries and strawberries.

Marshmallow Kebabs with Mars Bar Sauce

SERVES 6

• Definitely one for a sweet tooth, this is a brilliant addition to the Chocoholics' Bar, or just a really simple barbecue pudding to serve up for fun on its own.

2 Mars Bars
150ml double cream
2 packs marshmallows
20 x 15cm bamboo skewers, soaked for at least 30 minutes

To make the sauce This sauce is cooked in a bain marie, or a bowl over a pan of hot water, so you will need to find a mixing bowl that fits snugly over one of your saucepans. Chop the Mars Bars into 1cm pieces and place in the bowl with the cream. Pour an inch of water into the bain marie saucepan and bring to a bare simmer. Place the bowl over the hot water and leave the Mars Bar pieces to melt in the heating cream. The finished result will not be entirely smooth, but this is part of its charm.

For the marshmallows Skewer two marshmallows onto each skewer.

Barbecue The barbecue grill needs to be at least at medium heat. Clean and lightly oil the rack. Grill the marshmallow skewers for a total of 30–40 seconds, watching like a hawk, as they melt very quickly. Turn them once within this short time.

To serve Serve the kebabs immediately onto small plates for your sweet-toothed guests, directing them to the Mars Bar Sauce for drizzling.

Balsamic Strawberries and Ice Cream

SERVES 6

• Here's something slightly different to put together after a day at the pick-your-own. Strawberries and raspberries are the best for balsamic treatment. The vinegar brings out the flavour of the fruit. Try and get hold of an aged balsamic vinegar which is heavier and sweeter. If the fruit is not fully ripe and sweet, then you may need to add more sugar.

1.2kg ripe sweet strawberries, washed and hulled
1 tbsp aged balsamic vinegar
2 tbsp caster sugar
good quality vanilla ice cream

Toss the berries in a bowl with the vinegar and sugar. Cover and leave in the fridge for 2 hours until the berries are softened slightly and have produced a rich sweet-sour berry syrup. Serve with scoops of ice cream.

Tips Substitute some of the strawberries for raspberries, blueberries and blackberries if they are in season.

Grilled Pineapple with Vodka and Cracked Black Pepper

SERVES 6

• For Blistering, pineapple is the king of barbecue fruits. If you can get hold of the 'Supersweet' variety of pineapple then you are truly onto a winner. These are almost as good as the sensational ripe fruit you commonly buy in far-flung places such as India or Thailand.
• Refrigerate for one hour before grilling.

1 large ripe pineapple
6 tbsp vodka (flavour of your choice)
$\frac{1}{2}$ tsp cracked black pepper

To prepare the pineapple Cut off the top and bottom of the pineapple and place on a chopping board, flat bottom downwards. Using a large serrated-edged knife cut off the skin in long strips, from top to bottom, and work round the pineapple until all the skin is removed. The flesh will be studded with eyes of deeply imbedded skin. Cut these out with the point of a sharp kitchen knife. Slice the pineapple into quarters through the hard core and then slice out the core. Transfer the quarters to a plate and splash over the vodka. Sprinkle over the pepper. Cover and refrigerate for an hour.

Barbecue Preheat the grill to medium-high, or 'sizzle' temperature. Clean and lightly oil the rack. Grill the pineapple quarters for 4-5 minutes on each side until charring and caramelised.

To serve Transfer the grilled pineapple to a chopping board and slice into two-bite-size chunks. Transfer to a serving plate and skewer each piece with a bamboo skewer. Serve warm.

Grilled Pineapple with Rum and Maple Syrup

SERVES 6

• We think that pineapple is such a winner, that we couldn't resist adding a second recipe. Again, use the sweetest of pineapples, but if you do find that the pineapple is disappointingly under-ripe, then this recipe is pretty forgiving.

• Refrigerate for one hour before grilling.

1 large ripe pineapple
6 tbsp rum
3 tbsp maple syrup

extra maple syrup
double cream, to taste

To prepare the pineapple Cut off the top and bottom of the pineapple and place on a chopping board, flat bottom downwards. Using a large serrated-edged knife cut off the skin in long strips, from top to bottom, and work round the pineapple until all the skin is removed. The flesh will be studded with eyes of deeply imbedded skin. Cut these out with the point of a sharp kitchen knife. Slice the pineapple into quarters through the hard core and then slice out the core. Transfer the quarters to a plate and splash over the rum and maple syrup. Cover and refrigerate for an hour.

Barbecue Preheat the grill to medium–high, or 'sizzle' temperature. Clean and lightly oil the rack. Grill the pineapple quarters for 4–5 minutes on each side until charring and caramelised.

To serve Transfer the grilled pineapple to a chopping board and slice into two-bite-size chunks. Transfer to a serving plate and skewer each piece with a bamboo skewer. Serve warm with extra maple syrup and cream.

Pineapple is the king of barbecue fruits.

Baked Caramel Calvados Apples with Muscavado Sugar served with Calvados Caramel Sauce

SERVES 6

- Apples baked in a wood-fired oven are a dream. You could also try this recipe on the barbecue, with the stuffed fruit wrapped up in a treble layer of strong foil.
- The sauce is fantastic, but if you want the easy life, just serve the baked apples with crème fraiche, whipped cream or ice cream.
- You can stuff the apples and make the sauce a day ahead. Reheat the sauce in a double boiler or bain marie.

6 medium-sized cooking apples, or firm tart English apples, such as Coxes

For the stuffing
3 tbsp Muscavado, or dark brown sugar
3 tbsp sultanas
1/4 tsp freshly grated nutmeg
1/4 tsp ground allspice (optional)
110g cold butter cut into 1 cm dice

To bake
6 good splashes of Calvados or brandy

For the Calvados Caramel Sauce
350ml water
350g sugar
180ml double cream
150ml Calvados (or brandy or rum)

To prepare the apples Using an apple corer, or a small sharp knife, cut out the apple core. It doesn't matter if you lose a little of the apple, as you need to make room for the stuffing.

To stuff the apples Mix together the stuffing ingredients and pack the stuffing down into the hollowed apples.

To make the sauce Stir together the water and the sugar in a small saucepan. Place on a medium heat and dissolve the sugar, stirring from time to time. Once dissolved, bring to the boil and simmer, not stirring, until the syrup turns a golden amber colour. Take off the heat and stir in a couple of tablespoons of the cream, taking care as with the heat of the syrup, the mixture may spit and bubble up. Slowly and carefully, add the rest of the cream and then the Calvados.

Barbecue Preheat the grill to medium. Wrap the apples individually in a triple layer of strong foil measuring approximately 22cm square. Splash a tablespoon of Calvados into each parcel before crimping the tops like 6 foil money bags. Place on the grill and cook for 25–30 minutes, or until the apple has softened through and the sugar and butter has caramelised. You may be using a barbecue that is slowly cooling down, so timings vary dramatically. You may find that placing the wrapped apples directly into the embers is the best way to finish the baking process.

To Wood-roast Light your wood-fired oven and get up to heat as described on p24. Place the stuffed apples in a lightly buttered terracotta, or oven–proof dish that accommodates the apples snugly. Splash over the Calvados and bake on the trivet in a moderately hot oven for 15–20 minutes. If the apples are taking too much colour, cover them with a layer of foil and place them on the base of the oven at the front.

To serve Remove the baked apples carefully from the foil or dish and plate individually. Spoon the Calvados Caramel Sauce over the apples and serve straight away.

Roasted Stone Fruits

The summer is the season of gluts. Prices of soft fruits plummet as quality goes up. Wood-roasted stone fruits present sufficient reason on their own to invest in a wood-fired oven. Any ripe fruit halved into an ovenproof dish, sprinkled with sugar and whatever booze you fancy and popped in the wood-fired oven caramelise beautifully. Serve with cream and you're away. So easy, so elegant and so delicious.

In addition to the following, try ripe figs with grappa and Mascarpone mixed with cream and a little icing sugar.

Wood-roasted Apricots or Peaches with Amaretto, Toasted Almonds, Amaretti Biscuits and Double Cream

- Easier than pie in the wood-fired oven, and when ripe, sensational. They have a short season, but do try to get hold of white-fleshed peaches if you can. You may choose to add a little more sugar to the apricots.

To roast the peaches or apricots
6 peaches or 12 apricots, halved and destoned.
3 tbsp Amaretto liqueur
2 tbsp soft brown sugar

To serve
paper-wrapped Amaretti biscuits
2 tbsp toasted flaked almonds
250ml double cream, lightly whipped
1 tbsp sugar to add to the cream (optional)

To prepare the fruit for wood-roasting
Place the peach or apricot halves in a terracotta dish, cut-side-up, spoon over the Amaretto and sprinkle over the sugar.

To wood-roast Light the oven and bring up to temperature. Place the dish of fruit on the trivet and roast the apricots for 5-7 minutes and the peaches for 9-10 minutes, or until softening and caramelised. If the fruit is browning too quickly, transfer it to the floor of the oven, or cover with foil. Cook time varies widely according to the size and ripeness of the plums.

To barbecue Preheat the grill to medium-high, or 'sizzle' temperature. Be sure that the grill is cleaned and lightly oiled. Grill the peach or apricot halves, flesh-side-down for 3-4 minutes, or until charred and caramelising. Transfer the fruit halves to an oven-proof dish, flesh-side-up, or in three layers of strong foil measuring about 30cm square, crunched up around the edges to prevent any juice from escaping, Pour over the Amaretto and sprinkle over the sugar and place dish or foil package back on the grill. Cook for a further 5-6 minutes. Cook time varies widely according to the size and ripeness of the plums.

To serve If you have used a terracotta or other attractive oven-proof dish, scatter the hot roasted fruit with toasted almonds and place the dish in front of your guests next to a jug of double cream (sweetened if desired). Scatter wrapped Amaretti biscuits around the table. They'll soon get the idea.

Wood-roast Plums with Rosemary Red Wine Sauce And Cream

- Fruit that has had the chance to ripen naturally on the tree is sweeter then shop-bought. If you are lucky enough to have a plum tree in your garden, then in late August and early September, you're n for a treat. If you are using shop-bought plums, you may choose to add a little more sugar.
- The Rosemary Red Wine Sauce is delicious with the roast plums, but unnecessary if you use fresh plums from your own tree. The flavour of the plums and the juice they produce is so tantalising, that you need no more than a spoonful of heavy cream to set them off to perfection.

To roast the plums
1kg ripe plums, halved and de-stoned
4 tbsp water
2 tbsp soft brown sugar
1 tsp cinnamon (optional)
2 sprigs rosemary

For the sauce
400ml red wine
2 tbsp sugar
1 small sprig rosemary
1 vanilla pod, split in half lengthways
75g cold butter, finely diced

To serve
250ml cream or crème fraiche

To prepare the plums for wood-roasting
Place the plum halves in a terracotta dish, cut-side-up and spoon over the water. Mix the sugar with the cinnamon, if using, and scatter it over the fruit. Tuck the sprigs of rosemary in between the plums.

To wood-roast Light the oven and bring up to temperature. Place the dish of plums on the trivet and roast for 5-10 minutes, or until softening and caramelised. If the fruit is browning too quickly, transfer it to the floor of the oven, or cover with foil. Cook time varies widely according to the size and ripeness of the plums.

To prepare the plums for the barbecue
Mix the sugar with the cinnamon and scatter it over the bottom of the ovenproof dish. Place the plums flesh-side-down onto the sugar, splash over the water and tuck around the rosemary sprigs.

To barbecue Preheat the grill to medium-high or 'sizzle' temperature. Place the dish directly onto the coals to caramelise the sugar and fruit. Once the liquid is into the caramelisation stage, bring the dish back onto the grill bars, cover with a sheet of foil to trap in the steam and cook for a further 3-4 minutes, or until the fruit has softened. Cook time varies widely according to the size and ripeness of the plums.

For the sauce Pour the red wine, into a small saucepan and stir in the sugar with the rosemary and vanilla pod. Bring to the boil and reduce the volume by half. Strain the sauce into a bowl through a sieve and rinse out the pan. Return the reduced wine to the pan and scrape in the seeds from the vanilla pod, whisking to break them up. Bring the reduction back to the boil and take off the heat. Whisk in the pieces of butter a couple at a time, waiting until they emulsify before adding more.

To serve Plate up the plums, drizzle over some Rosemary Red Wine Sauce and some cream or crème fraiche and serve with thin shortbread biscuits.

Index

Suppliers we use and recommend

Macken Bros **020 8994 2646**

The one and only Rodney Macken, his brother Jimmy and all the lads at the shop in Chiswick, London have been supplying us with fabulous meat for years and always with a smile! Do visit their shop at Turnham Green Terrace, Chiswisk W4.

Andreas Georghiou & Co. **020 8995 0140**

Right across the road from Mackens is this great vegetables shop. Run by Andrew, his shop is always overflowing with the finest seasonal fruits and veg.

Hyams and Cockerton **020 7622 1167**

The family business run by Christian and his brother Blaire always supply quality produce and take us out for top lunches!

Villagers Fine Sausages **020 8325 5475**

Based in Beckenham, Kent, Ron makes award-winning sausages and people at Blistering are forever commenting on the cocktail ones. He has even been on *The Generation Game*! Mail order available. Take a look at www.englishsausages.com.

Macleod Forestry **01494 882 901**

Donald has been making his night time deliveries to us in London for years supplying us with the finest charcoal. Check out www.donlogs.com.

New London Wine **020 7622 2220**

Battersea-based Christopher Wells and Martin supply us with a great selection all year round. Check out www.newlondonwine.com

Alfa Pils **020 7622 3000**

The official Blistering house beer as tried and tested at Danny's Bar.

La Cuisiniere **020 7223 4487**

Not only did they supply us for this book, but this fabulous shop in Battersea, London is a must for quality kitchenware. Have a look at www.la-cuisiniere.co.uk.

Jacqueline Edge **020 7229 1172**

We have been buying from Jacqueline for years because not only do we like her superb selection ranging from Burmese Barbecues to umbrellas, but everything always stands up to the battering it gets during every Blistering season. Check out www.jacquelineedge.com.

Persepolis **020 7639 8007**

A great range of Persian foods, spices, teas, herbs etc and artefacts on Peckham High Street in London. Great for sumac and saffron. www.foratasteofpersia.com

Sayell Foods **020 7256 1080**

Based in Hoxton, London, Wendy and Jim introduced good quality, cheap Spanish Olive Oil to the catering world years ago. They now run an impressive, adventurous business supplying delicious and interesting Spanish foods, terracotta and ceramics. Great for saffron, chorizo, olive oil and so on. Check out www.sayellfoods.co.uk

SMB Foods **020 8693 7792**

A terrific high street delicatessen on Lordship Lane in East Dulwich. Great selection of jars, bottles and spices from all over the world. Fascinating selection of great quality fruit and vegetables.

Talad Thai **020 8789 8084**

Based in Putney, London, visit here for a comprehensive range of fresh and packaged Thai and other oriental ingredients. They also have some great value kitchen equipment in stock. Check out the stone pestle and mortars.

FC Soper Fishmongers **020 7639 9729**

A magnificent purveyor of fresh and frozen fish in Nunhead, South East London. Jason at Sopers introduced us to the joys of gilthead bream.

Reza Patisserie **020 7602 3674**

Nuts, seeds, spices and freshly baked pastries. The best pistachios in town. Based at 345 High Street Kensington, London..

Le Marrakech **020 8964 8307**

Top-notch Moroccan ingredients in Notting Hill.

Dadu's Cash and Carry **020 8672 4984**

Don't even think of buying your spices at the supermarket; the mark-up is extraordinary. Find your local Asian store and stock up on cumin, coriander, turmeric, garlic powder and the rest at bargain prices. For a fantastic selection of Indian and African ingredients, visit Dadu's, a veritable treasure trove on Tooting High Street.

Blistering Thanks

Sue at Reynards • Glenda, David and Kevin at Capital Express • Jori White and all her team • John, Jeremy and George at Direct Designs • Paul and Margaret at Blistering Beehive Ltd • John and Dorothy Weatherell for holding it all together • Russell at Box Products for delivering the goods • Damion and Margaret's for all the glitter! • Henry, Jo, Jack and Olive and all the Sri Lankan Crew • Our Ma's and Pa's for all of their inspiration and encouragement • Peter Drown • Gren and Neil at West Norfolk • Sally 'Dobo' Dobson • Jones Hire • Myles at Select First • Dave Salami Betteridge for literally thousands of photos • Jody and Simon at Bridges • Chamberlen for the introduction • Martin and Nicola at Cardale for all their great designs • All the lads at Farnborough • Pat King, Jonathan and Lorraine Seaward, Fifth Element, Zest, Lillingstone Associates and all those party planners who have had the faith to use us • Klaus and Christiane König • Jon, Matt, Meg and Little Meg at Absolute Press • The New Generation BB Crew – Billy, Fin, Tess Marnie, Mattie and Jake • And last, but not least, our gorgeous wives, Kate and Sophie, for their support and belief in us.

And thanks to the BB Crew – Past and Present

El Fred, Manu and Ronnie, Vid, Andy 'Camberwell Carrot' Porter, Cooki, Ninja Chef Asman, Davlova Watson, Mark Adonis Wright, Jason Wasabi Kennedy, Little Neil, Jason Curruthers, Gavin 'Chaud Devant' Murrey, Adam 'Danger Chef,' Mazzer, Vickey, Ranga Jo, Taffi Jones, Andy Gordon, Kiwi James for all his help with the book, Nuwanski (oh yeah!), Louise, Noodles, Camilla, Lee Smith, Bonnie and Fay, Viv, Chessytiana Jameson, Hillary, Marie, Genius, Shazza, Richard, Sparky Marky, Stan the Man, Steve Shaw, Lenny, Scroffy, Pikey Chris, Driftwood, Ray, Elli, Ivan, Benfolds and Jayhundis (happy retirement!), Danny 'Whodini' Wild for the perfect Pavlovas and all his help with this book, anyone else we have forgotten, and all those chefs, waiting staff and managers who have passed through the books over the years! A big 'aaaaaaaaah yeah' to you all!

Nige and Tim

About the authors

Kate Tunnicliff has worked in food marketing and advertising, restaurant management and as a chef for three years. She has also appeared in the BBC series *Hot Chefs*, and has styled food for various magazines and TV programmes and for films such as *The Fifth Element* and *Evita*. In 1993 she set up her own catering business. She is a well-respected food writer.

Nigel Tunnicliff entered the catering industry at the ripe old age of 14. Years of hard graft saw him work his way up to the position of Head Chef at the Dolphin Hotel, Poole. Eight years of living and working in foreign lands far and wide provided him with a wealth of culinary experience. He returned to the UK to work for some of the finest catering companies around. For several years, he ran a celebrated food stall at Glastonbury Rock Festival, and this led to a meeting with **Tim Reeves**. Tim started work in the music business with Virgin Records in 1988. He went on to set up his own dance label, Tomato Records, and then went into management. A career change saw him start work at the Chapel Pub in the west of London, one of the earlier great gastro pubs. There he became reacquainted with Nigel, who he had previously worked with selling falafels at Glastonbury. Nigel offered Tim a job as an assistant chef at Lodge Catering, where he was Head Chef. After two years of working together, they developed their idea to set up a specialist al fresco catering company....